W9-CHP-526

# 150 Best Bathroom Ideas

# 150 Best Bathroom Ideas

COLLINS DESIGN

*An Imprint of HarperCollins Publishers*

HarperCollins books may be purchased for educational, business, or sales promotional use.
For information, please write: Special Markets Department, HarperCollins*Publishers*,
10 East 53rd Street, New York, NY 10022.

First published in 2008 by:
Collins Design
*An Imprint of* HarperCollins*Publishers*
10 East 53rd Street
New York, NY 10022
Tel.: (212) 207-7000
Fax: (212) 207-7654
collinsdesign@harpercollins.com
www.harpercollins.com

Distributed throughout the world by:
HarperCollins*Publishers*
10 East 53rd Street
New York, NY 10022
Fax: (212) 207-7654

Executive editor:
Paco Asensio

Editorial coordination:
Simone R. Schleifer

Assistant editor coordinator:
Aitana Lleonart

Editor and texts:
Daniela Santos Quartino

Art director:
Mireia Casanovas Soley

Design and layout coordination:
Claudia Martínez Alonso

Layout:
Cristina Simó

Library of Congress Control Number: 2008944053

ISBN: 978-0-06-149362-1

Printed in Spain
First Printing, 2009

Contents

# Introduction

In recent years, few rooms have undergone such a radical transformation as the bathroom. Bathrooms have gone from being one of the most neglected rooms in the house to a central feature of modern living. In the past, a bathroom was exclusively for daily hygiene and therefore its décor and location within a house was secondary to all other rooms. The growing culture of well-being has dramatically changed this concept. Our quest to escape from the frantic pace of life and to redefine the limits between what is private and public has generated new needs. And the answers to these needs lie in this space: the bathroom.

Today, traditional functions are maintained but advances in technology have allowed our bathrooms to reach unprecedented levels of sophistication, and new relaxation features have converted them into real private spas.

Bathroom designs have become pivotal. Even in the smallest and most modest bathrooms, new finishes and elements have been introduced to integrate this space into the personality of the rest of the dwelling. Bathroom designs therefore echo many different styles. This is possible thanks to the wide range of furnishings and fittings that have come onto the market to satisfy the growing importance of this space. In fact, many prestigious architects and designers have wanted to leave their stamp on this space by designing collections of bathroom fittings, fixtures and furniture.

These new aesthetics have helped the bathroom to move beyond its traditional sphere and to take up new spaces in the house. En-suite bathrooms or separate guest bathrooms are no longer the exclusive domain of deluxe dwellings.

The bathrooms in the following pages bear witness to this radical transformation and serve as an inspiration for those designing a room that has the power to change our quality of life.

# NATURAL

## Villa Berkel

In order to make sure that the thick woods surrounding the house does not block natural light from entering, three of the four façades are made entirely of glass. The rooms requiring greater privacy, such as the bathroom, are located in the part of the building opposite the entrance. A rectangular mirror of water and the garden's vegetation give those living in the house the sensation of being in full contact with nature.

Architect: Architentenbureau Paul de Ruiter
Location: Veenendaal, The Netherlands
Date of construction: 2005
Photography: Pieter Kers

The bathroom, like all rooms in the house, looks directly out onto the garden located at the south of the site.

Floor Plan

1. Entrance
2. Kitchen
3. Living room
4. Study
5. Bedroom
6. Master room
7. Master bathroom
8. Pond
9. Terrace

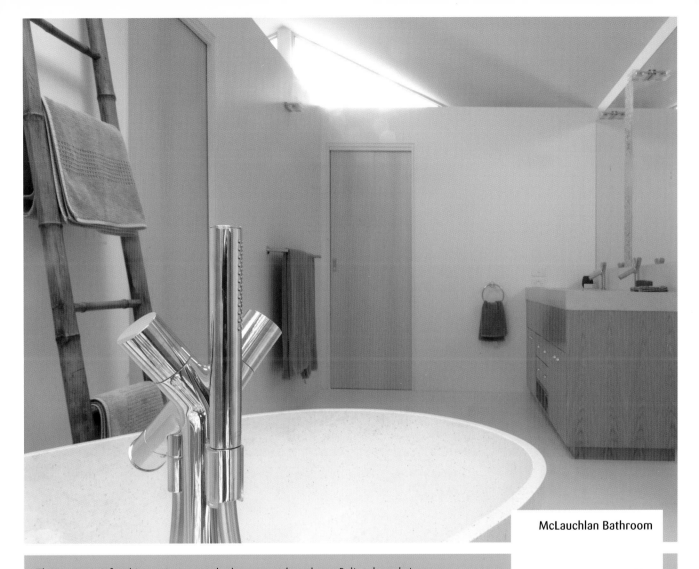

**McLauchlan Bathroom**

The inspiration for this spacious, open bathroom was based on a Bali style and gives those living in this house in Australia the sensation of living in a tropical climate. The main feature is the natural light that floods in through the skylights and the enormous window that looks out onto the garden. The shower is discreetly hidden away behind columns covered in limestone tiles. The same material is used for the floor, except for the bath area which is covered in pebble stone tiles.

Architect: Rob McLauchlan
Location: Mornington Peninsula, Australia
Date of construction: 2006
Photography: Shania Shegedyn

2

The bamboo ladder serves
as a towel rail and emphasizes
the natural element of this
bathroom.

3

The round bathtub was
bought in Bali, as was the
handcrafted natural stone
wash-hand basin.

The range of materials used in this bathroom have been selected to fit in with the natural surroundings of the house. The space is separated from the master bedroom by a sliding wall. The freestanding bathtub appears to merge into the landscape and the shower is in close contact with the exterior.

Architect: Stephen Jolson
Location: Mornington Peninsula, Australia
Date of construction: 2003
Photography: Shania Shegedyn

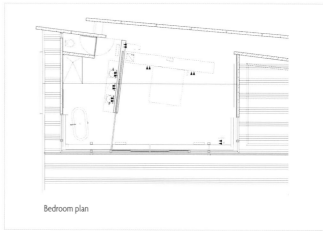

Bedroom plan

SHINOKI.

294-BELLINO PACIFIC PALISADES

LUXE BY ALBIC.

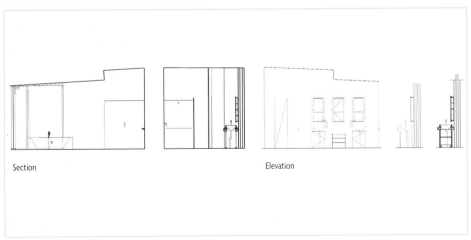

Section

Elevation

## 4

Bamboo wood has been used to fit out the bathroom as it is very moisture-resistant.

**Rubin Residence
Master Bath**

Architect: McIntosh Poris
Associates

Location: Michigan, USA

Date of construction: 2007

Photography: Kevin Bauman

Located on the edge of a ravine, this family home is characterized by its total integration with the surroundings. From the inside, the house virtually opens up to the natural surroundings through the wide back windows. In this context, the master bathroom has views that give those living there the sensation of being in the middle of the woods. Inside, the focal points are the "his and her" washbasins with their onyx vanity tops and a double-sided mirror hanging from the ceiling.

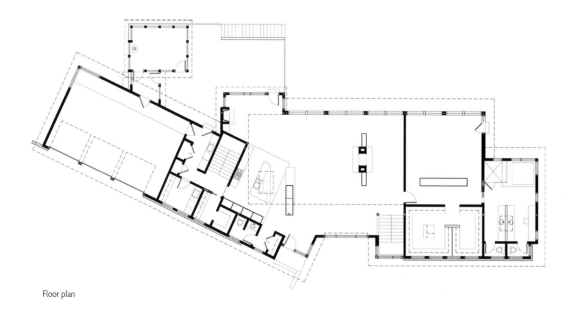

Floor plan

5

The lighting located under the vanity top creates a sense of intimacy.

6

The ergonomic lounger in the glass shower area provides a comfortable seat and almost could be mistaken for a work of art.

Vantomme

When the exterior views offer so much, the only alternative on the inside is to maximize this privileged situation. For this reason, the sculptural bathtub occupies the entire space along the fixed glass wall that replaces the exterior wall. The shower is marked by a transparent screen so as not to obstruct the natural light, and the wooden floor provides the warmth necessary to turn this room into a sanctuary of well-being.

Architect: Anthony Duffeleer/FRAP
Location: Zwevegem, Belgium
Date of construction: 2008
Photography: Luc Roymans

7

The shower screen is
hardly noticeable as it has
no metallic joints.

**Blue Earthenware Bath**

In contrast to most en-suite bathrooms, this one has been distributed along the length and width of the main bedroom. The bath and the window occupy the complementary space of the balcony and make the most of the sea views. At the other end, the washbasin fixture consists of a wooden console with a rustic finish. The hand basin in antique style contrasts with the modern minimalist-style faucets. Behind the partition, the toilets are located and another hand basin.

Designer: C&C Studio
Place: Alicante, Spain
Date of construction: 2007
Photography: José Luis
Hausmann

## 8

In order to maintain the bedroom style, a wooden console was used on which to rest the washbasin.

## Ses Oliveres Country Estate

Architect: Lizarriturry Tuneu Arquitectura

Place: El Empordá, Spain

Date of construction: 2007

Photography: José Luis Hausmann

This house, surrounded by vast olive plantations and wheat fields, has been designed in harmony with its rural environment without, however, dispensing with the amenities of modern life. The bathroom, like the rest of the house, is in natural clay. The distribution of this space seeks maximum functionality and so is distributed in three areas separated by internal partitions. The toilets, washbasins and shower are located adjacent to a picture window with views of nature.

## 9

The faucets and accessories on the wall help to save space for the basin surface area.

The design of this bathroom, which is part of a family home, prioritizes functionality and quality of materials. The toilet area is located behind a partition which separates it from the bathing area. There are two fitted washbasins inset to a marble surface beneath a frameless mirror. A slight slope defines the shower with wood floor. Further back, the bath is situated, as the owners did not want to dispense with one in order to bathe the children.

## Cabrils House

Designer: SR Constructors
Place: Barcelona, Spain
Date of construction: 2006
Photography: José Luis Hausmann

## 10

The treated wood on the
shower floor provides warmth
to a bathroom dominated by
cool finishes.

11

The stone slab finish on the wall of the washbasins creates an interesting visual contrast, in addition to being ideal for repelling dampness.

This en-suite bathroom in a main bedroom makes the most of the structural element dividing the two areas. A low half wall houses the washbasin stand with storage space at the back. Above, the double-sided mirror increases the feeling of space in the bedroom.

Architect: Jordi Galí Estudi
Place: Madrid, Spain
Date of construction: 2007
Photography: Jordi Miralles

## 12

The washbasin fixture is provided with a transparent apron on the top to protect the bedroom from water splashes.

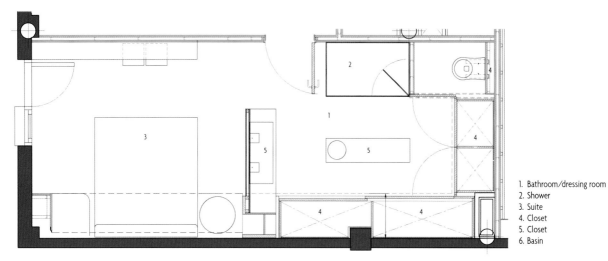

Floor plan

1. Bathroom/dressing room
2. Shower
3. Suite
4. Closet
5. Closet
6. Basin

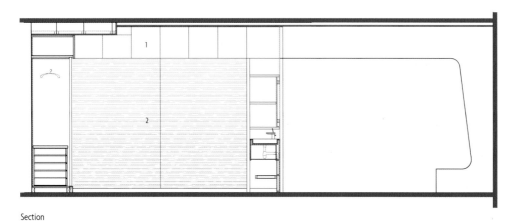

Section

1. Lacquered doors
2. Closet

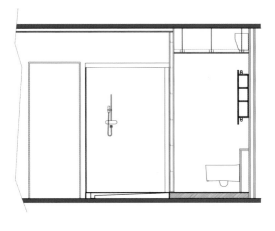

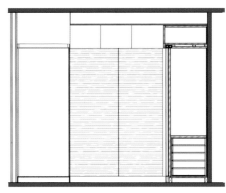

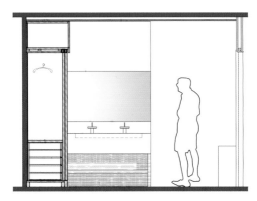

Sections

13

The shower has a hydro massage column and is equipped for color therapy.

**Geis Loft**

The main bedroom of this renovated duplex apartment has been designed as a unique space containing the bathroom and is equipped for relaxation. The dressing area and countertop has been placed in the space and also fulfils the function of a bed head. The toilets and the shower were constructed on the back wall of the house.

Architect: Slade Architecture
Place: New York, United States
Date of construction: 2006
Photography: Jordi Miralles

First floor plan

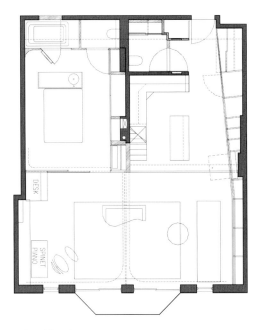

Second floor plan

14

This washbasin front, formed by a white countertop and spacious drawers without handles, provides an extensive storage area.

**Suite with Charm**

This bathroom was designed to create a natural, timeless atmosphere with colors and materials that emanate calm. Therefore, natural colors have been used, stone, marble and unvarnished wood. The shower zone is a main feature with its large shower heads and thermostatic faucets. The vintage furniture and the washbasins, decorated by the Ramón Soler company, lend the room a Bohemian air reminiscent of Provence.

Designer: Carmen Barasona
Place: Barcelona, Spain
Date of construction: 2007
Photography: Jordi Canosa,
Mauricio Salinas

## 15

To avoid altering one of the brick walls, aged metal pipes were used to channel cabling while at the same time serving as a decorative element.

## Ron Ron House

The master bedroom's en-suite bathroom has been designed in order to make the most of the breathtaking views over the Pacific Ocean. The bathroom is divided into two zones: one of these areas is dedicated to the wash area, marked out by a decking and fitted out with a Philippe Stark bathtub, and the other is the toilet area. Although both areas are separate, they are linked by a glass door, which allows an abundance of natural light to enter.

Architect: Victor Cañas
Location: Guanacoste,
Costa Rica
Date of construction: 2007
Photography: Jordi Miralles

## 16

Polished cement, wood and glass are the predominant materials used in the master bedroom's en-suite bathroom.

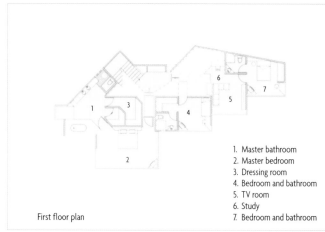

First floor plan

1. Master bathroom
2. Master bedroom
3. Dressing room
4. Bedroom and bathroom
5. TV room
6. Study
7. Bedroom and bathroom

## 17

Decking is an excellent way
to mark out space in en-suite
bathrooms.

**Portas Novas House**

The open plan structure of the bathroom is typical with all housing located in a dry tropical climate zone. The bathroom is divided into two areas. One area holds the toilet and the other area holds the shower/bath area. The two areas are closed off for maximum privacy. The skylights and pebble gardens in this zone help create an element of harmony between the outside and the inside of the house.

Architect: Victor Cañas
Location: Guanacaste, Costa Rica
Date of construction: 2005
Photography: Jordi Miralles

## 18

The cement wall contains the wash-hand basin and two double-sided, made-to-measure mirrors.

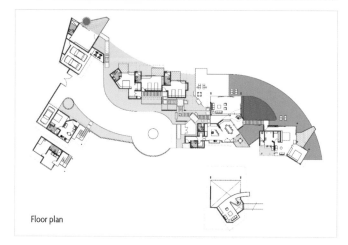

Floor plan

Design: Carmen Barasona / © Jordi Canosa ; Mauricio Salinas

# NATURAL

## Inspirations

# SPA

Södra Ängby

This space, almost like a temple dedicated to one's well-being, shows the best of Swedish traditions and includes a shower, bath and sauna. The solid block of black granite in the center of the 340-square-foot bathroom contains the bath and in the part behind, a wooden wash-hand basin. In order to create a sensation of spaciousness, both the shower and the sauna are marked out by a screen and glass walls.

Architect: Rahel Belatchew Arkitektur
Location: Stockholm, Sweden
Date of construction: 2007
Photography: RB Arkitektur

## 19

The long wooden bench in front of the bathtub links the sauna with the rest of the space.

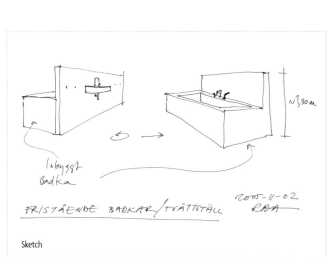

Inbyggt Badka

FRISTÅENDE BADKAR / TVÄTTSTÄLL

2005-11-02
RBA

~1,30 m

Sketch

## 20

The wash-hand basin and
the bathtub are in one single
structure in order to make
good use of the sanitary
fixtures.

## 21

Two large steps, which can also serve as benches, lead to the bath.

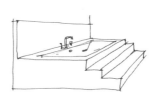

FRISTÅENDE INBYGGT
BADKAR MED STEG

2005-11-02
RBA

Sketch

## Pierrefeu House

The open plan bathroom integrated in the main bedroom takes in spectacular views of the Mediterranean. With this configuration the bath has a central position. On the back wall the washbasin has been fitted on a wooden shelf with a chest of drawers and a mirror. The shower has a glass back partition with rounded pebbles as flooring.

Architect: Octavio Mestre
Place: Mallorca, Spain
Date of construction: 2005
Photography: Jordi Miralles

## 22

The shelves inset into the wall save space without altering the area's aesthetics.

23

With simple lines and brilliant finish, the faucets and appliances are entirely in keeping with this contemporary bathroom.

**Bathroom of an Architect**

The bathroom occupies part of a large square space of clean lines in the roof of an old house. This space, measuring 37 x 8.5 ft, has been designed with a minimalist concept in both shape and color. The brilliant white emanating from light tubes on the 1.6-ft-wide wall panels is scarcely noticeable against the pure white of the walls. The bathtub plays an outstanding role, not only because of its central position, but because it shines in different colors when the lights are off.

Architect: **Kevin Van Volcem**
Location: **Bruges, Belgium**
Date of construction: **2007**
Photography: **Luc Roymans**

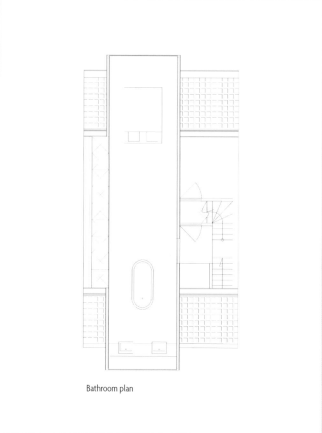

Bathroom plan

## 24

The bathroom is situated in a box-shaped structure together with the master bedroom.

# 25

Half the panels include
storage space.

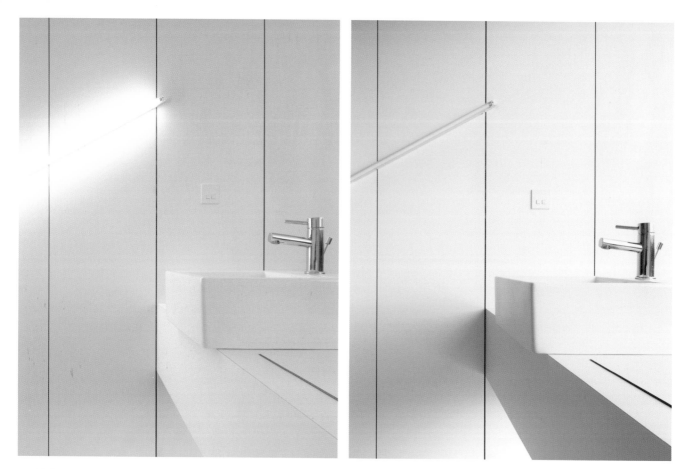

## 26

The bathtub, made by the company WET, is transparent and contains a LED light system that makes it glow in different colors.

**XL-Loft**

This 2,660-square-foot loft contains a main box containing the bedroom and dressing room. This structure is surrounded by a glass wall which defines the kitchen dining area, storage and the bathroom. Making use of this high level of exposed areas, the bathroom design prioritizes empty space. In this way the shower, the toilets and the storage were housed in a black box so that they are concealed from the hallway.

Architect: Nico Heysse
Place: Brussels, Belgium
Date of construction: 2005
Photography: Laurent Brandajs

## 27

The lack of volume transfers emphasis to the lighting which bathes the bathroom in a variety of colors.

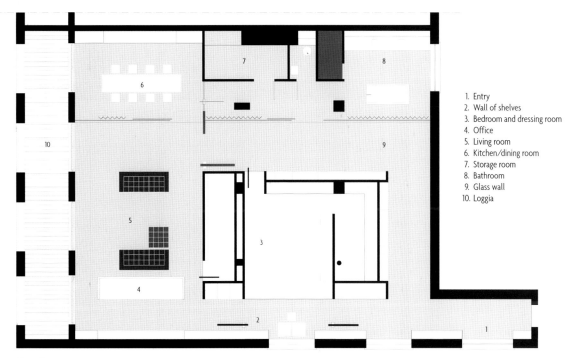

Floor plan

1. Entry
2. Wall of shelves
3. Bedroom and dressing room
4. Office
5. Living room
6. Kitchen/dining room
7. Storage room
8. Bathroom
9. Glass wall
10. Loggia

28

On one side the ceiling has been lowered to fit with the black structure which houses the toilets and the shower.

This en-suite bathroom is located to one side of the bedroom. While the en-suite communicates with the bedroom via a vertical opaque glass panel which can be raised or lowered, it also is directly linked to the Japanese garden through two windows: a horizontal one over the Jacuzzi bath, and a vertical one going up from the floor to the ceiling in the shower area.

### West Melbourne Warehouse

Architect: Nicholas Murray Architects
Location: Melbourne, Australia
Date of construction: 2008
Photography: Shania Shegedyn

## 29

This bathroom uses rain water which is stored in ten thousand liter tanks.

## 30

The use of glass with embossed water droplets assures the privacy of the toilet area.

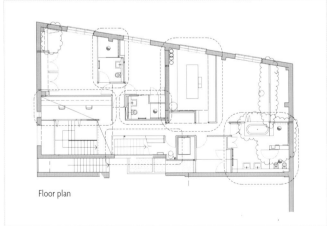

Floor plan

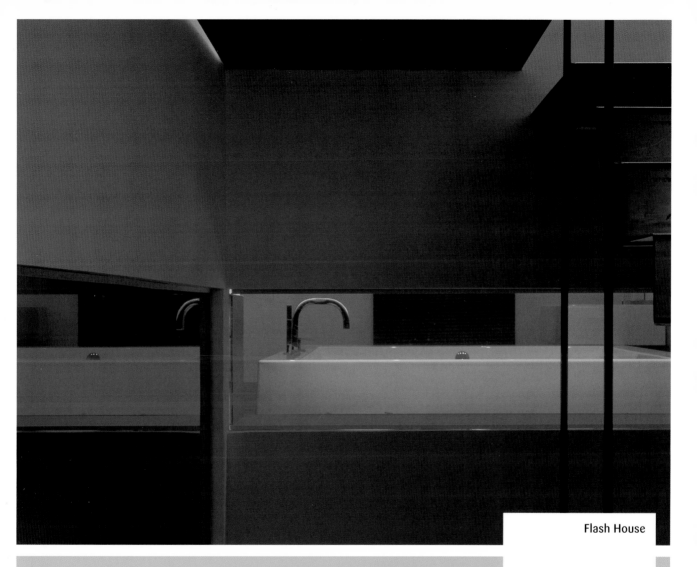

A mixture of finishes, an absence of ornamentation and a very functional distribution are the main features of the en-suite bathroom in this three-story house. The space, which can be seen from the stairs, forms part of the "night area" consisting of a closet, a large shower with a deck, the sanitary fixtures and a small Kos swimming pool/bath with an adjoining wash-hand basin.

Architect: Filippo Bombace
Location: Rome, Italy
Date of construction: 2006
Photography: Luigi Filetici

Section

Suite plan

1. Bed
2. Dressing room
3. Service area
4. Shower
5. Pool

## 31

Pure lines and soft colors favor those spaces destined for relaxation.

### Harmony

The perfect combination where traditional meets modern. This bathroom is located in the guest area of a skyscraper apartment in Tokyo. The bathroom area takes up most of the 160 sq ft apartment. The pure and elemental lines of architecture are complemented by the minimalist aesthetics, such as spacious surfaces of gray stone and pink glass that invite one to relax.

Architect: Gwenael Nicolas/
Curiosity
Location: Tokyo, Japan
Date of construction: 2008
Photography: Daici Ano

32

The pool/bath has a tray to
collect any overflow water.

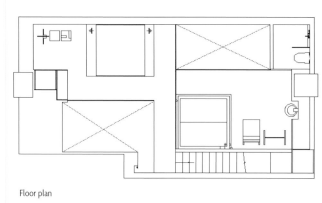

Floor plan

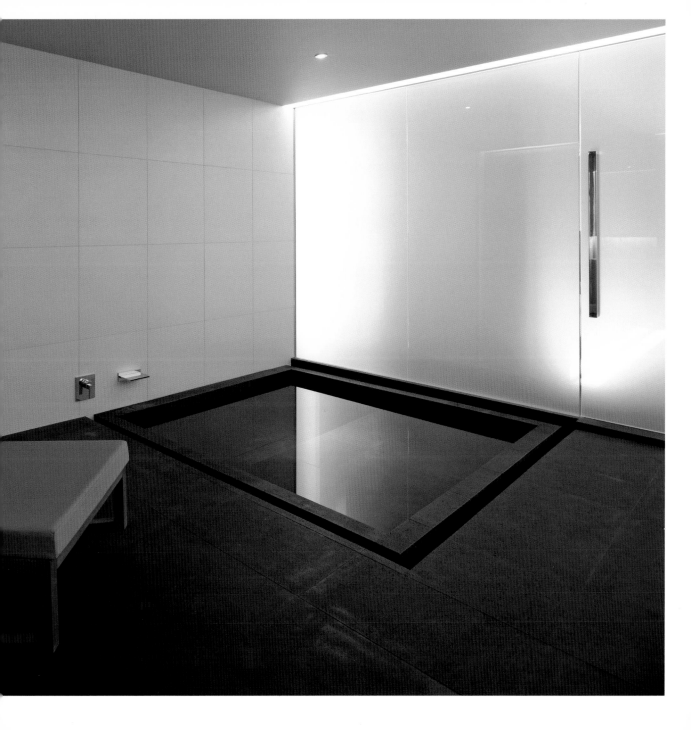

**Bathroom with a View**

Architects: **EX-IT Architecture**
Location: **Beveren, Belgium**
Date of construction: **2005**
Photography: **Luc Roymans,
Nike Bourgeois**

This house is located in a residential area surrounded by agricultural lands and consequently has been designed to take advantage of the views. As a result, the glass walls appear to be live paintings reflecting the ever-changing outside scenery. The design of the bathroom follows the same lines and makes the most of the scenery from all corners of the room, including the sauna.

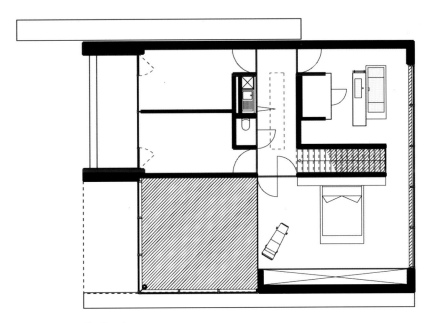

First floor plan

## 33

The polished stone wash-hand basin and the bath form an attractive combination of volumes and contrasts.

The bathroom design blends vintage elements with other more contemporary items. The vibrant green of the walls brings a contemporary touch, contrasting with the traditional hexagonal floor mosaics. To keep the space as clear and uncluttered as possible, the shower/sauna is situated apart in an area accessed through a transparent glass door.

**4 Centre Market**

Architects: Sixx Design
Place: New York, United States
Date of construction: 2004
Photography: Luc Roymans

## 34

Vintage details such as the
Moroccan-style lamp and the
antique poster on the doors
leading to the bedroom create
a cosy atmosphere.

The restoration of this house was carried out by maintaining the original structure intact and strengthening it with new and modern structures. The bathroom on the first floor maintains the same singularity as prior to the restoration, but it has a new distribution owing to a new mosaic tiled panel which serves as a support to the bathtub. A private spa, with sauna, toilet area and shower has been installed in the stone-covered vault on the second floor.

Architect: **Landau + Kindelbacher**
Location: **Munich, Germany**
Date of construction: **2007**
Photography: **Christian Hacker**

## 35

The tiles, in brown and red tones, maintain the heat of the sauna area and give a personal touch to this private spa.

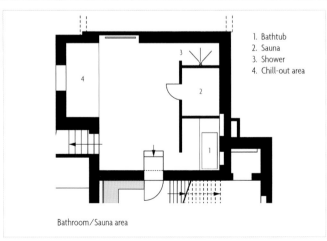

1. Bathtub
2. Sauna
3. Shower
4. Chill-out area

Bathroom/Sauna area

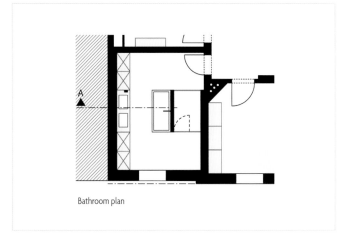

Bathroom plan

© Agape Design

# SPA

Inspirations

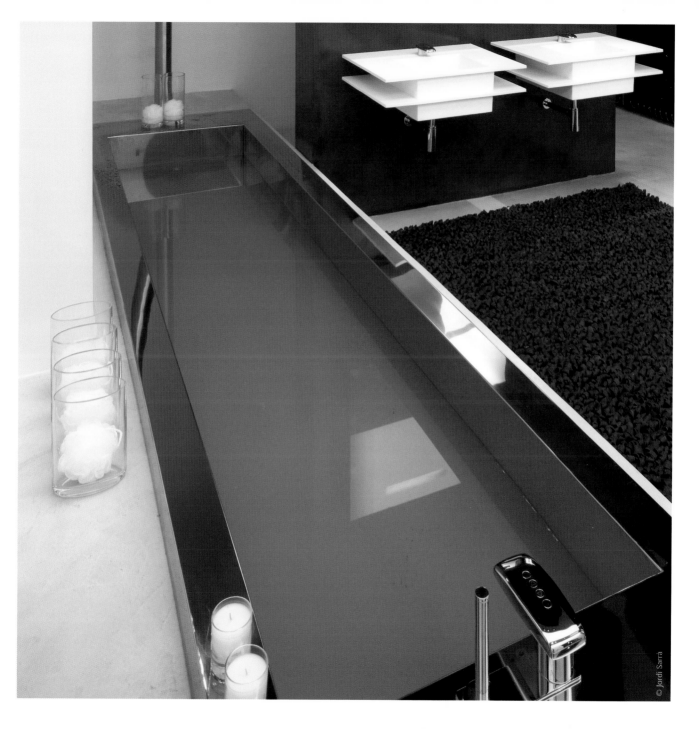

# MODERN-DAY LUXURY

**Glamorous En-suite**

A once gloomy room in the heart of a Victorian-style terrace has been transformed into a place glowing with reflected light. The space, used exclusively by the owner of the house (a woman with two small children), radiates exuberance and femininity. It leads onto a dressing room and a balcony with a deck. To give a sensation of greater space and to reflect the light, the designer covered the walls leading onto the dressing room with mirrors and gave the floor a polished finish.

Architect: Jean-Pierre Heurteau
Location: Melbourne, Australia
Date of construction: 2007
Photography: Shania Shegedyn

## 36

The minimalistic style of the freestanding bathtub contrasts with the Victorian chest of drawers covered in glass and the velvet-upholstered ottoman seat.

1. Bathtub
2. Washbasin
3. Console
4. Door to hall
5. Dressing room
6. Garden deck
7. Bedroom door

Bathroom plan

# 37

The lacquered floor protects
it from the damp and provides
luminosity.

The architects have captured the essence of present-day minimalism while remodeling this house built in the '60s. All the surfaces are mainly neutral and natural tones. The bathroom seems to be sculptured directly out of stone owing to the 35 x 35 inch Elba marble tiles covering the floor, walls and the central block where the bathtub is located.

Architect: **Coy + Yiontis Architects**
Location: **Melbourne, Australia**
Date of construction: **2007**
Photography: **Shania Shegedyn**

## 38

Ornamentation has been kept
to a minimum in order to
emphasize the natural beauty
of the stone used for
the tiling.

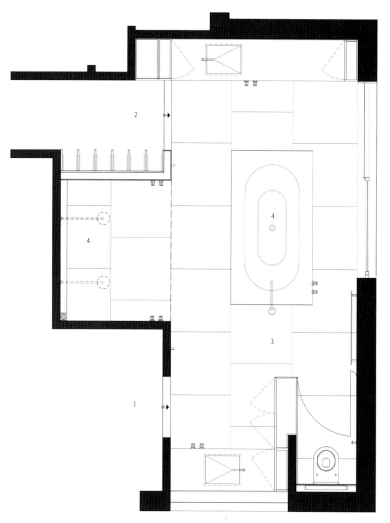

1. Entry
2. Entry 2
3. En-suite
4. Bathtub shower

Floor plan

## 39

The use of a contrasting piece of furniture which is unconnected to the bathroom creates a unique ambience.

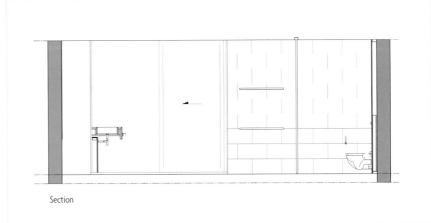

Section

**Windsor Loft**

The bathroom has been designed in the same way as one in a small luxury hotel, integrated into the bedroom but at the same time maintaining a certain amount of independence. The ceiling and the sliding glass windows protect it from climate changes and the mirror situated on the facing wall increases the natural light. When the sliding doors are left open the bathroom blends into the patio and is transformed into a sanctuary of relaxation.

Architect: Architects EAT
Location: Melbourne, Australia
Date of construction: 2006
Photography: Shania Shegedyn

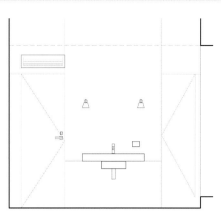

North internal elevation

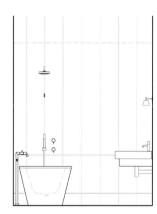

West internal elevation

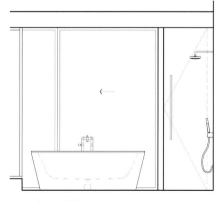

South internal elevation

## 40

The ceiling over the bathtub is glass and leads to relaxing baths under the sun or moon.

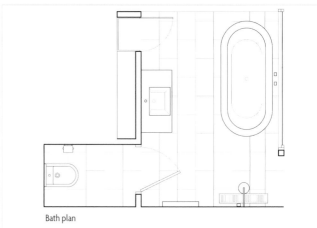

Bath plan

This bathroom is able to cope with the dark finishes due to the abundant light emanating from two main sources: the window which looks out onto the exterior; and on the other side, the transparent glass wall situated in the stairwell which reaches the upstairs level where the bathroom shares space with an office.

Architect: Alonso Balaguer
y Arquitectos Asociados
Place: Barcelona, Spain
Date of construction: 2006
Photography: Jordi Miralles

## 41

The shower walls do not reach the ceiling in order to let light enter.

42

The parquet flooring provides warmth to this atmosphere dominated by anthracite grey stone and steel.

House L4

L4 is a family home built on land with huge trees. The building is set on a triangular piece of land and its materials are designed to create a fusion of textures with the environment. The bathrooms are an illustration of this with travertine and onyx finishes, creating an organic feel.

Architect: Jaime Rouillon Architecture
Place: San José, Costa Rica
Date of construction: 2002
Photography: Jordi Miralles

# 43

The light has been strategically situated to highlight the material textures.

## Light Bathroom

The bathroom has been organized in a separate area from the bedroom, but remains visually integrated. This is possible due to the enormous glass window which stands out at night with its brilliant amber edges. The same effect is repeated on the bedroom ceiling, and around the bath.

Architect: **MoHen Design**
Place: **Shangai, China**
Date of construction: **2007**
Photography: **MoHen Design**

44

Within the transparent glass enclosure the water zone is located with bath and shower.

1. Hallway
2. Dining room
3. Living room
4. Kitchen
5. Study room
6. Master room
7. Master bathroom
8. Guest room
9. Bathroom
10. Balcony

Floor plan

## 45

The shower has been installed
in a column with seating.
The floor is formed by round
pieces with spaces for
drainage.

**Gemdale Green Town**

Chinese culture tends to avoid black for superstitious reasons. However, the designers took a risk and used this color as a basis for the bathroom in this home. They applied it to the walls, using granite facing, and lacquered finishes combining it with the pure white of the fixtures and fittings. The bathroom connects with the main bedroom through two passageways, in one of which a dressing room has been installed.

Designer: **One Plus Partnership**
Place: **Wu Han, China**
Date of construction: **2006**
Photography: **Gabriel Leung**

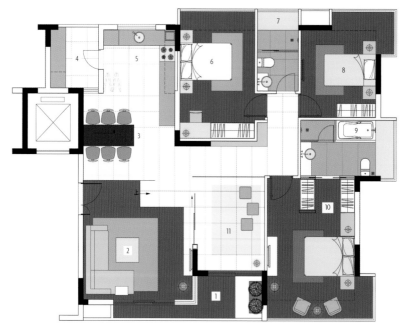

1. Balcony
2. Living
3. Dining room
4. Utility
5. Kitchen
6. Bedroom
7. Power room
8. Kid´s room
9. Master bathroom
10. Master bedroom
11. Game room

Plan

46

The yellow light generates a dramatic effect in this area dominated by stone, stainless steel and lacquered paint.

This home has been renovated in a loft style in the public areas without sacrificing the generous spacious areas for those needing greater privacy. The house has two bathrooms. The main bedroom bathroom has a large dressing area in white silestone with a washbasin running from point to point. The vertical mirrors providing indirect light are supported on the wengue wood top. The guest bathroom is also provided with a white custom-made counter surface with inset washbasin.

Architect: Meritxell Cuartero
Cavallé/Dt6 Arquitectes
Place: Barcelona, Spain
Date of construction: 2004
Photography: Jordi Miralles

Elevation

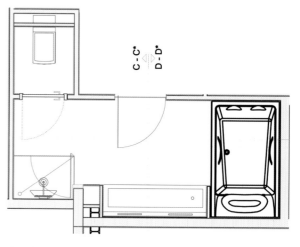

Floor plan

# 47

The indirect light and the white surface establish an aesthetic connection between the two bathrooms in the home.

Space Winding

Integrated in the main bedroom, this bathroom designed in contemporary Oriental style conveys the same sensation of calm and relaxation as the rest of the house. The shower and the toilets are contained within a glass enclosure Continuity with the other parts of the home is evident in the bedroom color scheme that extends to the bathroom. On a background of somber colors and fine materials, the minor decorative details are key items in defining the particular character of this space.

Architect: MoHen Design
Place: Shangai, China
Date of construction: 2007
Photography: MoHen Design

## 48

The lighting is distributed
in small points of light which
contributes to creating
an intimate atmosphere.

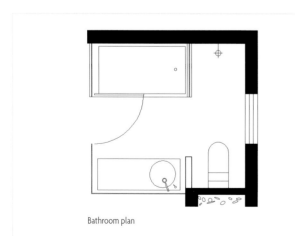

Bathroom plan

# MODERN-DAY LUXURY

## Inspirations

# UPDATED CLASSIC

As soon as you enter the main bedroom in this apartment the first thing you see is a black polished stone surface with a washbasin and faucets with pure lines and geometric forms. The remaining bathroom fittings are contained in a black opaque glass enclosure. The shower also contributes to the dominant color scheme with its mosaic finish, the shower plate and even the splash curtain.

Designer: Jorge Queralt
Place: Barcelona, Spain
Date of construction: 2006
Photography: Jordi Miralles

## 49

Functionality and aesthetics: the narrow shelf situated above the toilet enables pictures to be displayed.

The color black has an undeniable visual impact and a great effect on ambience. Combined with the color white, it provides the ultimate in contrast, as is the case in this bathroom. The bathroom fixtures and the bathtub are the main features and there is a maximum use of space.

**House De Meester-Haentjens**

Architect: **Verdickt & Verdickt Architects**
Location: **Bechem, Belgium**
Date of construction: **2008**
Photography: **Luc Roymans**

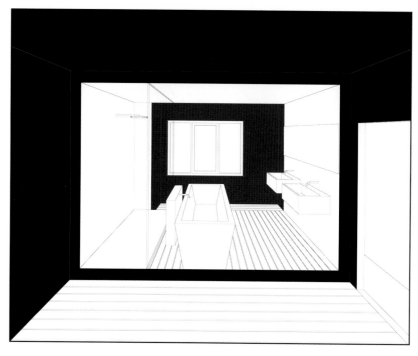

Sketch

## 50

The extreme color contrast
and the simple shapes used
give this classic bathroom
a contemporary style.

**ZZ House**

In order to give a greater sense of space, the architect decided on the limited use of materials in this small Roman-style attic. The chromatically severe and noble marble is the main feature of the bathroom. The main bathroom is situated next to the bedroom, behind a large sliding wooden door. A small interior glass window at floor level discloses the bathroom from the bedroom and allows a glimpse of the shower deck.

Architect: **Filippo Bombace**
Location: **Rome, Italy**
Date of construction: **2007**
Photography: **Luigi Filetici**

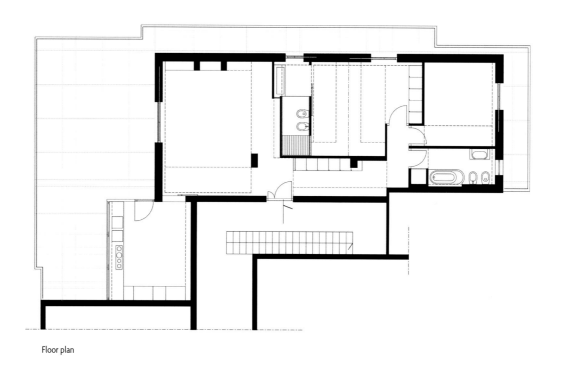

Floor plan

## 51

Indirect lighting offsets the coldness of the marble.

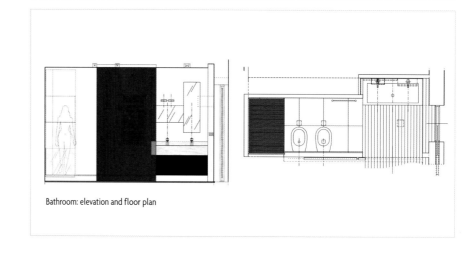

Bathroom: elevation and floor plan

## Rudy's House

This 4,300 sq ft house divided into three floors emanates comfort and tranquillity due to the natural fluidity of the spaces and the generous windows. Here the en-suite bathroom in the main bedroom is housed in a structure with a semi-transparent enclosure designed to provide more light. The combination of white mosaics, Carrara marble and stainless steel creates a contemporary atmosphere with classical elegance.

Architect: Yann Chu/Marais Design
Place: Taipei, Taiwan
Date of construction: 2006
Photography: Marc Gerritsen

## 52

The ceiling and part of the
walls of the bathroom are
translucent.

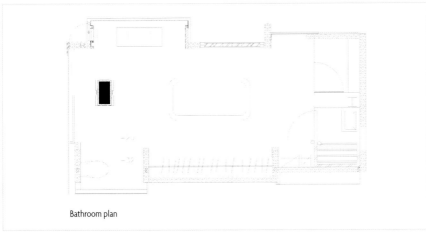

Bathroom plan

Following the minimalist style of the rest of this restored house, this bathroom is both simple and elegant. The current bathroom takes up the same amount of space as the previous bathroom, the only difference being that the architects have installed a partition wall that discreetly hides the showers. This new wall holds up the bathtub. The mirrored walls and the Calcutta marble cladding help to disperse the light that comes in through the small windows.

Architect: Nixon Tulloch Fortey
Architecture
Location: Victoria, Australia
Date of construction: 2008
Photography: Shania Shegedyn

## 53

To maximize space, the cupboards have been hidden behind the mirror panels.

Elevations

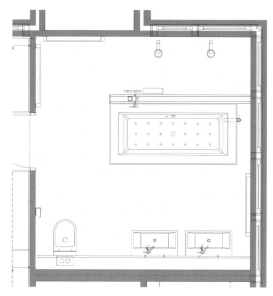

Bathroom plan

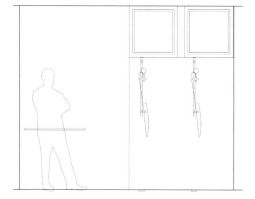

Elevation

**GZ Lake Villa**

This home's proximity to a lake inspired the designers to highlight the color blue in the various areas of the house. The specific exception to this are the bathrooms in golden neutral tones which provide a delicate contrast to dispel any risk of monotony.

Designer: **One Plus Partnership**
Place: **Guangzhou, China**
Date of construction: **2007**
Photography: **Gabriel Leung**

## 54

The extensive surfaces covered with mirrors provide lightness to the marble finished areas.

## Homage Hill Unit B

A large rectangular mirror defines the line separating this bathroom from the main bedroom, with an aesthetic and functional purpose. It consists of a rectangular component which turns on an axis. One side is a mirror, and the other side is finished in green with a small magnifying mirror inset.

Designer: **One Plus Partnership**
Place: **Shenzen, China**
Date of construction: **2005**
Photography: **Gabriel Leung**

## 55

The large rectangular mirror turns on an axis.

Floor plan

**Hotel Pershing Hall**

The sobriety and elegance conveyed by this bathroom has been achieved through the blend of contemporary design with mineral tones and fine materials. The luxury suite of this famous Parisian hotel has a marble and stone finish in the lower part of the walls and floor, and the rest of the surface is finished with grey and brown mosaics made by Bisazza. A personal touch is provided by the decorative details such as the unusual shape of the bath and the lamps over the washbasins.

Designer: Andrée Putman
Place: Paris, France
Date of construction: 2001
Photography: courtesy of Bisazza

## 56

The lamps reach the mirror and their reflection is duplicated, creating an interesting effect.

**Homage Hill**

The combination of multicolored mosaics forming borders adds a personalized touch to the bathroom. The bath is at floor level, which liberates the space visually. The lighting is strategically situated above the washbasin and the shower, creating an intimate atmosphere.

Designer: One Plus Partnership
Place: Shenzen, China
Date of construction: 2006
Photography: Gabriel Leung

## 57

The curtain rail follows the shape of the shower which is at floor level.

**Bathroom MarS Architects**

This bathroom was designed by its architects as a composition of shapes and levels. The shower and the bathtub form together just one transparent shape, which stands out against the dark oak floor. The frameless mirror is part of a composition on the Carrara marble wall and helps to increase the sense of space. The design conveys the utmost importance of the different finishes (oak, marble and plastics), unlike the ceiling where the cement has been left exposed.

Architect: **MarS Architects**
Location: **Vilvoorde, Belgium**
Date of construction: **2007**
Photography: **Luc Royman**

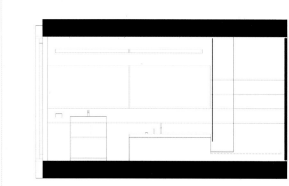

Elevation

## 58

The large window, which faces out onto the street, has an exterior aluminum curtain that regulates the bathroom's light.

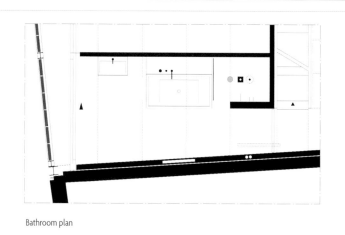

Bathroom plan

**South Melbourne House**

A timeless design transmits a sense of relaxation through the use of natural materials and clean architectural lines. The architects followed this guideline when they designed the three bathrooms—one of them en-suite—which are part of a recently restored, officially protected house.

Architect: Anna Vaughan Architects
Location: Melbourne, Australia
Date of construction: 2002
Photography: Simon Wood

## 59

A harmony of color tones
is essential to achieve a space
that invites relaxation.

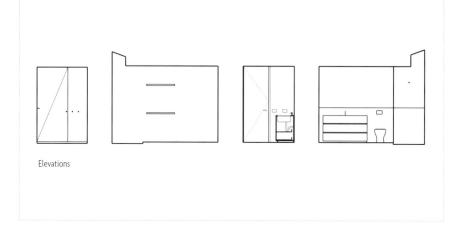

Elevations

Architect: **Filip Deslee**
Location: **Aarschot, Belgium**
Date of construction: **2007**
Photography: **Luc Roymans**

The architect introduced an attention-seeking element in this spacious 130 sq ft bathroom full of natural light. This is a turquoise-colored unit, which extends into a seat with drawers and has a lightweight appearance because it does not reach the floor. The wash-hand basin unit and the adjoining cupboards are at the same distance from the floor as the blue seat and together they form a single unit.

## 60

The presence of a contrasting
color bestows vitality to a
bathroom full of natural light.

© Marc Gerritsen

# UPDATED CLASSIC

## Inspirations

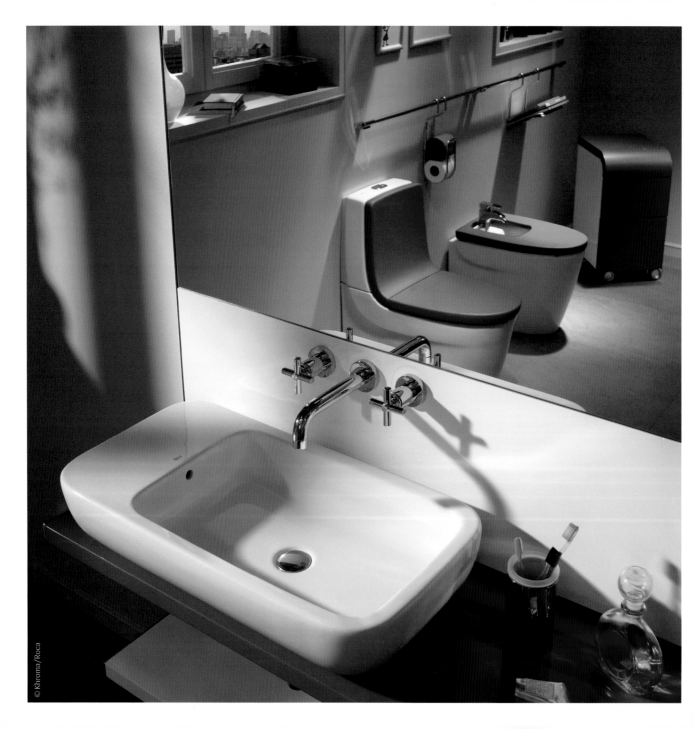

# CONTEMPORARY AVANT-GARDE

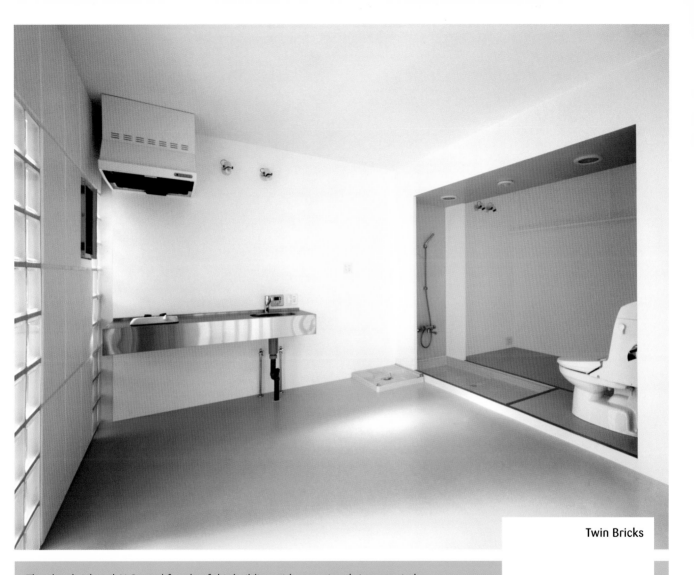

## Twin Bricks

The glass brick and ALC panel façade of this building with two wings brings to mind the famous computer game Tetris. Nowhere is the maximization of available square meters in each of the apartments as successful as in the bathrooms. The toilet and the shower share the same space in one of the interior openings. They have features to maximize privacy and are made to stand out through the use of color.

Architect: Atelier Tekuto
Location: Urawa, Japan
Date of construction: 2008
Photography: Makoto Yoshida

61

The kitchen sink is also used as the wash-hand basin in the bathroom.

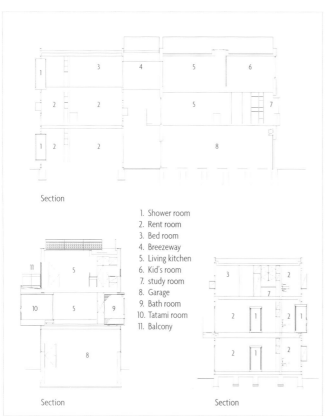

Section

1. Shower room
2. Rent room
3. Bed room
4. Breezeway
5. Living kitchen
6. Kid's room
7. study room
8. Garage
9. Bath room
10. Tatami room
11. Balcony

Section

Section

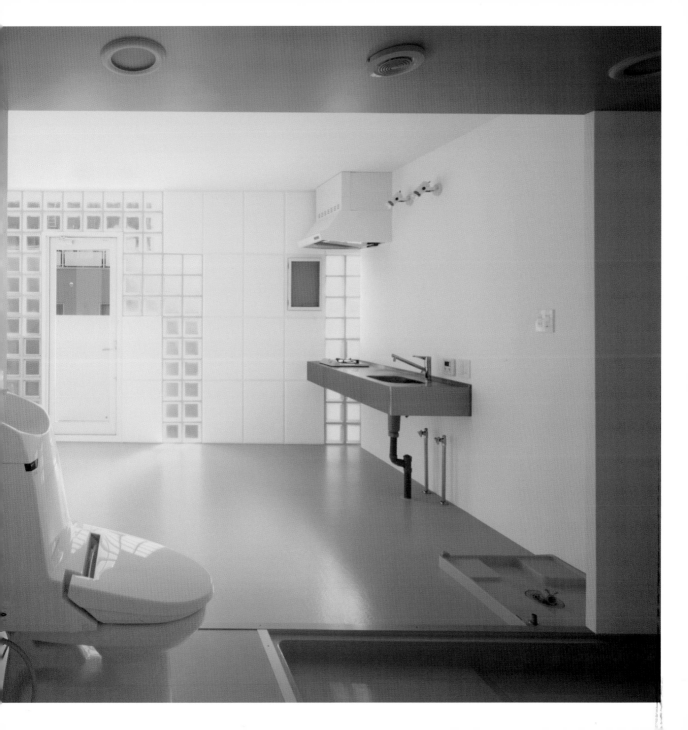

This three-story dwelling is the result of the extensive remodeling of an old warehouse. The rigidity of the original cement structure has been softened by a subtle play of lights, surfaces and internal and external spaces. In the same way, the glass bathroom located on the second floor is linked to the children's bedroom and lessens the concept of private and public spaces. The large marble vanity top ties the bathroom area to the rest area and establishes a visual counterpoint with the angles of the exterior wall.

Architect: Fougeron Architecture
Location: San Francisco, USA
Date of construction: 2007
Photography: Richard Barnes

## 62

The vanity top consists of the wash-hand basin and a series of elevated cabinets that create a greater sensation of space.

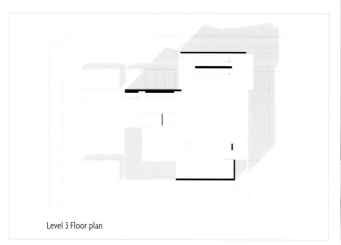

Level 3 Floor plan

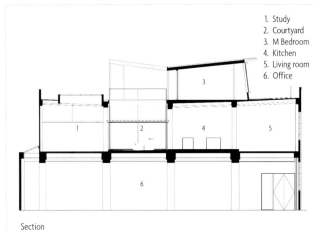

1. Study
2. Courtyard
3. M Bedroom
4. Kitchen
5. Living room
6. Office

Section

## Necklace House

Located in the countryside and surrounded by mountains, this house stretches out like a necklace with units linked together through small gardens. The bathroom is the only structure where, for reasons of privacy, the interior cannot be seen from the main garden. However, its metallic walls with 1,600 perforations, allow light to enter and create an almost magical ambience.

Architect: NAP Architects
Location: Yamagata, Japan
Date of construction: 2007
Photography: Daici Ano, NAP

63

The bathroom is located in a structure similar to a traditional house, and has 1,600 perforations.

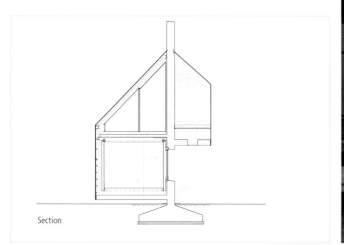

Section

**Skin Wall TV**

This triangular-shaped building houses a hairdresser on the first floor, the owners' residence on the second, and another living area for four people on the third floor. This particular bathroom is located on the upper floor encapsulated in a glass box. A few metal steps lead up to this structure which is raised a meter from the ground. The bathroom, which has a shower, toilets and a bathtub, is in the same area as the living room and the kitchen.

Architect: Atelier Tekuto
Location: Funabashi, China
Date of construction: 2007
Photography: Makoto Yoshida

## 64

As a creative touch, the bathroom is visible from the entrance of the house.

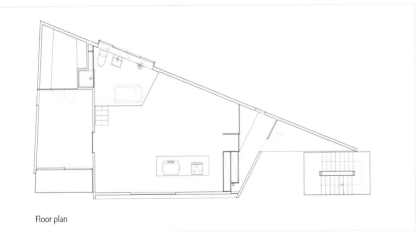

Floor plan

**Back to Black**

Integrated in a young person's bedroom, this bathroom is framed between transparent glass enclosures to make the most of the light entering from the windows of the main bedroom. An elongated skylight has also been installed in the wall of the washbasin and the mirror to facilitate ventilation. The finishings use the same chromatic range as in the bedroom.

Designer: **Luis Guillén**
Place: **Castelldefels, Spain**
Date of construction: **2007**
Photography: **José Luis Hausmann**

65

The toilet and the washbasin fixture are detached from the floor to increase the feeling of space.

## Guest Bathroom Pierrefeu

The en-suite bathroom in this Mallorcan guesthouse is a black and white composition which contrasts with the bedroom of which it is part. Like the varnished back wall, the bath and the washbasin are black and the bathroom fittings and the washbasin fixture are highlighted by the white purity of their forms. The mirror, which takes up the whole wall from floor to ceiling, visually extends the space.

Architect: Octavio Mestre
Place: Mallorca, Spain
Date of construction: 2005
Photography Jordi Miralles

## 66

The faucets and fittings are silver and are an ideal complement, in harmony with the two-color scheme of this bathroom.

## Nuria Amat House

The enormous challenge for the architect, who built this house on a cliff without changing it, is witnessed by the bare rock which forms part of the house in places. In the main bedroom the stone wall has been kept in its natural state, in order to locate the bathroom, which provides a contrast with its purity of color and form. The toilets and the dressing area have been distributed on the other side, behind a partition that separates the two areas.

Designer: Jordi Garcés
Place: Tamariu, Spain
Date of construction: 2006
Photography: Jordi Miralles

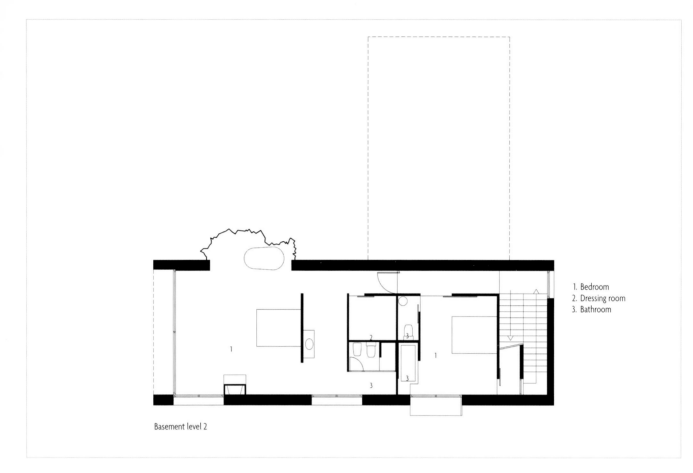

1. Bedroom
2. Dressing room
3. Bathroom

Basement level 2

67

The partition which separates the toilets from the bathroom does not reach the roof, thus keeping a connection between the two areas.

## 68

Freedom of design and
coexisting styles mark the
decorative tone.

**Tsai Residence**

The Tsai Residence is a combination of two units, one central area comprising bedroom, bathroom and sitting room, and another unit for guests. The main unit has a futuristic appearance. The space is defined by a white painted sheet of board which folds and lifts, acting as floor, wall and roof at the same time. The bathroom is encapsulated in one of the loops of the board. Although it is open at the sides, privacy is ensured due to its diagonal arrangement.

Architect: CJ Studio
Place: Taipei, Taiwan
Date of construction: 2007
Photography: Marc Gerritsen

## 69

The toilets, washbasins and showers were installed outside the capsule, in the external back wall of the bathroom.

When bathrooms take up space inside the bedroom, an attempt can be made to conceal them or conversely, a feature can be made of their presence. Such is the case of the en-suite bathroom which openly takes up the bed head, barely separated from the rest of the room by a glass panel. This also makes best use of the natural light from the windows of the main room.

Architect: CJ Studio
Place: Taipei, Taiwan
Date of construction: 2005
Photography: Marc Gerritsen

## 70

The cupboards and shelves
have been installed to one
side so that the main wall
is as minimalist as possible.

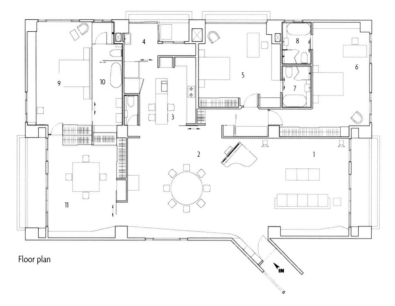

1. Living room
2. Dining room
3. Kitchen
4. Working area
5. Bedroom
6. Bedroom
7. Bathroom
8. Bathroom
9. Master bedroom
10. Bathroom
11. Dressing room

Floor plan

IN

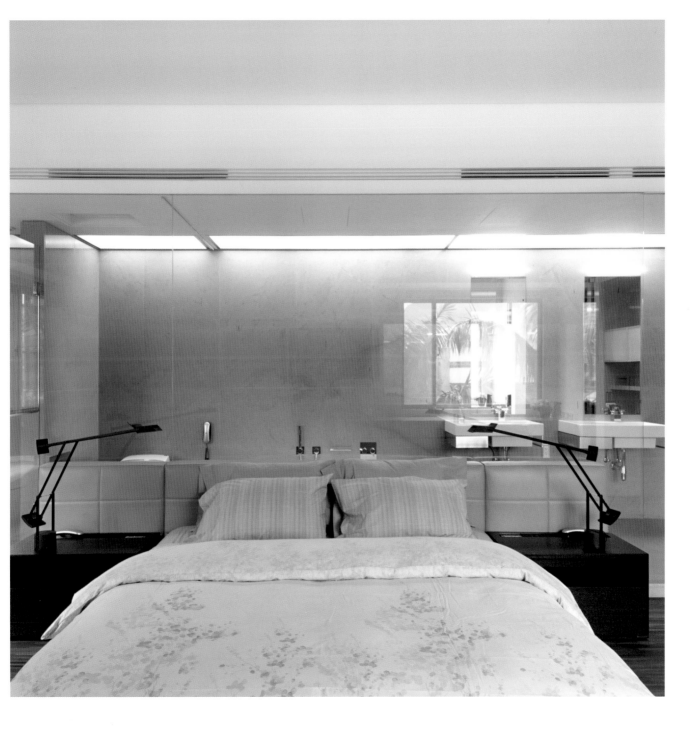

## Studio house garage
## Cadillac

Architect: García & Ruiz
Place: Madrid, Spain
Date of construction: 2007
Photography: Pedro Mmahamud

This home is a proposal for living cheek by jowl with your vehicle in Madrid.
The 750 sq ft of the former garage have been converted by means of a central fold
in a space with numerous and varied perspectives totally unconventional in design.
In this new type of home all the areas feature equally prominent. For this reason the
bathroom has eschewed the typical configuration and is deconstructed, occupying
various areas.

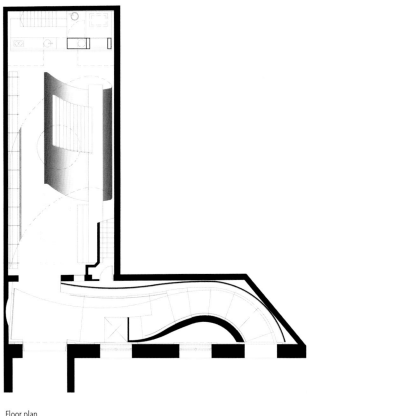

Floor plan

## 71

The toilet and hand basin have been located in different areas of the home.

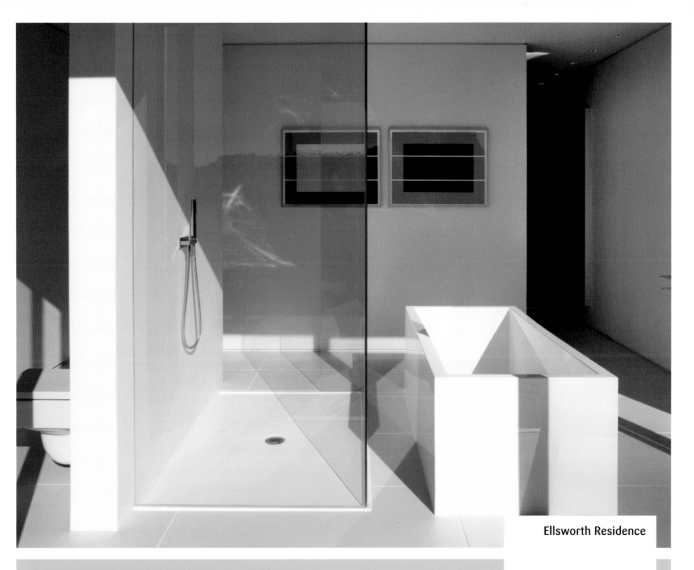

## Ellsworth Residence

The home is built in the desert in almost total isolation. Its design is open to the landscape which is set off in all its splendor through large picture windows in the façade. The bathroom in the guest bedroom is situated at one end of the house. The surfaces of the shower and the Corian bath (designed by Wetstyle) have invisible joints with a seamless effect that reinforces the purity of the overall design.

Designer: Michael P. Johnson Design Studios
Place: Arizona, USA
Date of construction: 2007
Photography: Bill Timmerman

Floor plan

1. Master suite
2. Master bath
3. Closet
4. Powder room
5. Kitchen
6. Dining

7. Cantilevered
   balcony
8. Living
9. Entry walk
10. Carport
11. Motorcourt

12. Mech.
13. Entry walk
14. Driveway
15. Terrace
16. Guest room
17. Guest bath

72

The partition, shower panel
and bath are aligned in a
central volume, around which
it is possible to move freely.

## Uptown

This bathroom, which is en suite in the main bedroom, is defined on the basis of a partition, giving the room an almost sculptural feeling. Inspired by the idea of a folio of paper, the design uses the fold as a surface for insetting the washbasin and the mirror. In order to reinforce the impact of this structure and to provide the bathroom with its own identity, color contrast has been used.

Designer: One Plus Partnership
Place: Shunde, China
Date of construction: 2008
Photography: Gabriel Leung

73

The two bathroom windows are practically unnoticeable due to the roller blinds of the same color as the wall.

# CONTEMPORARY AVANT-GARDE

## Inspirations

# CHIC

**Bathroom in Eixample**

Having renovated the home, the bathroom was designed in the area formerly occupied by the kitchen. The 97 sq ft of space were distributed into three zones defined by their different levels. Close to the entry door the dressing area was located, where warm materials predominate. A 9.8 inch slope marks access to the toilet area behind a partition which ensures privacy. The adjacent bath area is separated from the rest of the room by two plates of transparent glass and is situated at a higher level.

Designer: Jorge Subietas
Place: Barcelona, Spain
Date of construction: 2007
Photography: José Luis Hausmann

## 74

The made-to-measure
metal curtain which hangs
behind the bath filters
light and provides a touch
of sophistication.

## Joan Pons' Bathroom

This bathroom, located between the two bedrooms of the house, is accessed through a communal dressing room. As a separator for the two areas, a sliding glass door framed with welded iron has been installed. The toilet area is independent in that the shower is situated behind a transparent glass partition. The bath and the en-suite washbasin have the same burnished mortar finish as the walls. The teak flooring throughout the area has open joints in the shower area to collect water.

Architect: Joan Pons Forment
Place: Barcelona, Spain
Date of construction: 2007
Photography: José Luis Hausmann

## 75

An opening with fixed glass has been fitted in the wall separating the bathroom from the main bedroom.

## Orange Bathroom

Architect: Joan Dot
Place: Manlleu, Spain
Date of construction: 2007
Photography: José Luis Hausmann

Due to the reduced dimensions, this bathroom was designed to make the most of every inch of space. The transparent glass partition separating it from the bedroom ensures a feeling of space, although the area has its own windows for light and ventilation. The choice of bathroom accessories and fixtures was made on the basis of modernity and functionality. The flooring continues in the shower with a porcelain finish maintains the visual continuity of the area.

76

The color scheme reinforces the continuity between bathroom and bedroom.

## 77

The bathroom has a sliding
access door to save space.

## Green Bathroom

Designer: Pere Duran

Place: Barcelona, Spain

Date of construction: 2007

Photography: José Luis

Hausmann

This bathroom has been exclusively designed for the two children of the house with vibrant colors and simple and easily accessible furnishings. The green tiles set the informal tone of the area. The sliding doors and large drawer under the washbasin contribute to keeping the place tidy.

## 78

The textiles play a prominent role in the youthful aesthetics of this children's bathroom.

For functionality and pleasure, each of these six bathrooms of this three-story residential building has been designed with its own character. From the most informal and contemporary styles of bathroom with colored borders, to the most simple and classic of styles. An upper floor houses a "wellness area" with sauna, showers, and an adjoining interior sports court.

**Stadtvilla Pullach**

Architect: Landau + Kindelbacher
Location: Munich, Germany
Date of construction: 2008
Photography: Christian Hacker

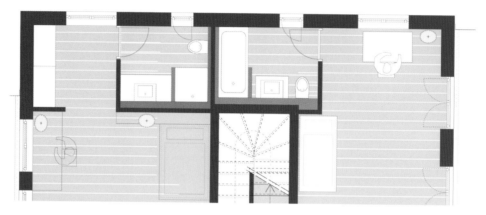

Bathroom first floor

79

Bisazza mosaics offer both
the design of wallpaper
and the advantages of a
waterproof material.

## 80

A television is situated behind the washbasin mirrors, and only becomes visible when it is switched on.

Bathroom first floor

81

All bathrooms have heated floors and walls.

82

The shower area is easily
visible by contrasting black
natural stone tiles.

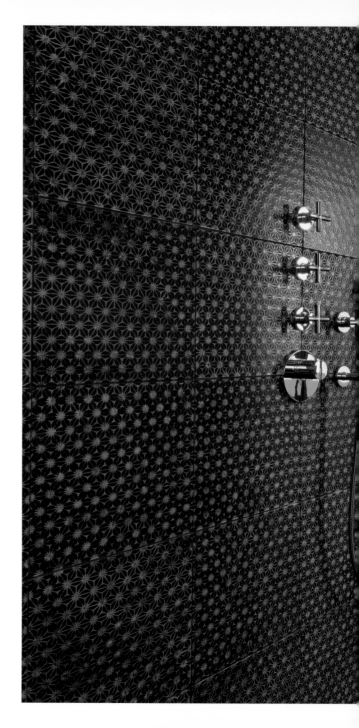

## Model House

The reduced space shared by the bedroom and the bathroom has made it necessary to enclose the bath in a box of translucent glass panels so that damp does not extend to the rest of the atmosphere. In addition to this physical barrier, the bathroom zone is identified by the mosaic finish. The same color was maintained for the rest of the surfaces of the residence, in keeping with the integrated whole.

Architect: CJ Studio
Place: Taipei, Taiwan
Date of construction: 2007
Photography: Marc Gerritsen

## 83

The intense light projects from the ceiling onto the bathroom surface and the mirrors take up the whole of one wall, defining the dressing area.

## The Black Apartment

The color black completely dominates this loft built for a famous New York publicist who wanted to feel "as if he was in a Shangai bar in his home." Instead of partition walls, the apartment has a series of thick curtains which create different ambiences. For this reason the bathroom is located near one of the structural walls—the only white wall in the house and where all the bathroom fixtures are situated. Steps lead up to the bathtub situated on a black mosaic tiled platform.

Designer: The Apartment
Location: New York, USA
Date of construction: 2005
Photography: Michael Weber

## 84

The built-in shelves in both the shower platform and the marble wall have no effect on the geometry of the bathroom and help to gain space.

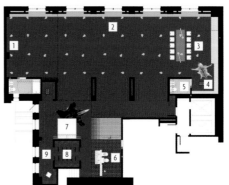

Floor plan

1. Library
2. Living room
3. Dining room
4. Kitchen
5. WC
6. Bathroom
7. Bedroom
8. Closet
9. Make-up room

### Chef

The designer has deliberately created an area that evokes memories of old-style kitchens with his dining room area. The bathroom is based on a wood-veneered structure in the form of a tube, which continues into the bedroom and forms part of the bed. The striking interior mosaic finish can be seen from outside through the curved amber glass walls.

Designer: **One Plus Partnership**
Place: **Shenzen, China**
Date of construction: **2007**
Photography: **Gabriel Leung**

## 85

The transparency of the bathroom has been used to show off the walls which are finished with attractively designed mosaics.

Floor plan

Suite number 1 of this private aparthotel maintains the structure and materials recycled from the former house. In this case, the bathroom is on the ground floor and is the first thing to be seen on entering the suite. The wall, covered with Bisazza "snowflake" mosaics, immediately attracts attention and defines the dressing area. The bath and the shower situated in the adjacent area provide a contrast, set in an area of smooth surfaces and natural tones.

Designer: Marcel Wanders, Karin Krautgartner
Place: Amsterdam, Holland
Date of construction: 2005
Photography: Alberto Ferrero

## 86

The style is also defined in details such as the industrial faucets for the washbasins and the shower, and the openings in the cupboard which are heart shaped.

## 87

The washbasin appears suspended in the air as the shelf that supports it is finished in the same way as the wall.

5 Centre Market

Architects: Sixx Design
Place: New York, USA
Date of construction: 2004
Photography: Luc Roymans

As well as being functional and practical, the contemporary style bathrooms have a decorative touch commensurate with the owner's personality. For this reason, despite the 258 sq ft occupied by the bathroom, the presence of different focal points created by various ornamental pieces changes the dimensions of the area, transforming it into a place of pleasure and relaxation.

## 88

The pure and minimalist
lines of the bathroom and
faucet contrast with the
antique-style chandelier.

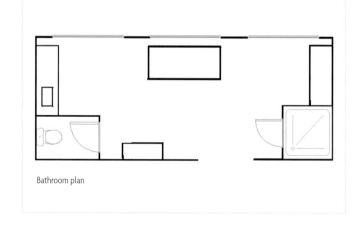

Bathroom plan

© Jordi Miralles

# CHIC

## Inspirations

Architect: Cream / © Cream

LASS DIE GROSSEN ELEMENTE
DIESEN ANBRECHENDEN TAG SEGNEN:

DIE ERDE MIT IHREM DUFT,
DAS WASSER MIT SEINEM GESCHMACK,
DAS FEUER MIT SEINEM LEUCHTEN,
DIE LUFT MIT IHRER BERÜHRUNG
UND DER RAUM MIT SEINEN TÖNEN.

# DESIGN CODE

# FURNISHINGS

© Pomme d'Or

© Smallbone of Devizes

89

Decorative elements have definitively defined bathrooms, creating personalized and attractive spaces.

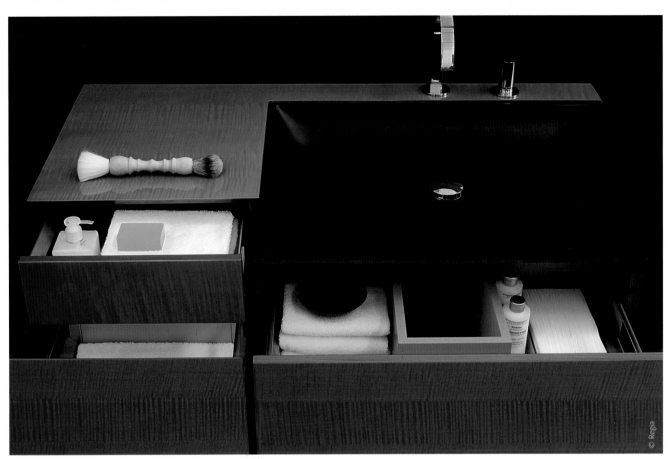

90

The contrast of colors and textures between the maple wood and the built-in basin is a decorative feature in itself.

© Keuco

91

The multiple drawers in this
unit with built-in washbasin
provide a practical solution to
the problem of how to store
daily-use products.

© Kohler

© Pomme d'Or

92

The drawers with rails and hidden spaces on the countertop help to optimize the space.

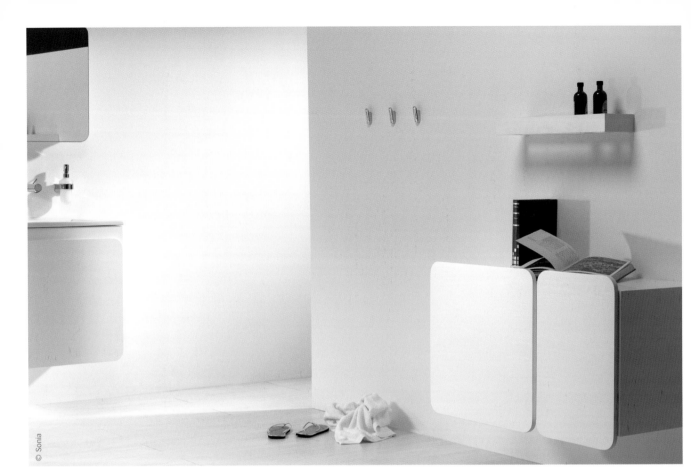

© Sonia

## 93

This add-on module creates a new storage area in the bathroom.

© Julien

## 94

The sliding cover of this unit
hides the WC, serves as a seat
and uncovers a storage space.

95

The interior lighting in this unit with glass blind is an attractive storage solution.

© Pomme d'Or

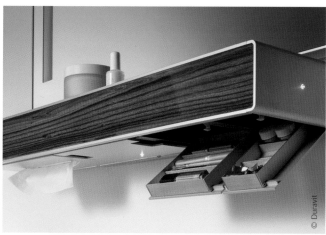

© Duravit

96

The limited range of colors in the furniture imbues the space with amplitude, serenity and sophistication.

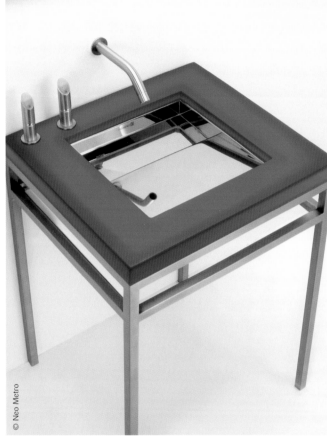

## 97

More suggestive
environments can be created
by using furniture such as this
stainless steel and resin unit
with interior light.

© Duravit

98

The furniture, with simple geometric lines, adapts snugly to all the spaces to optimize space.

© Boffi

## 99

The essence of the bathroom has changed. It has become a space to relax and therefore features new pieces such as this wood sun lounger.

© Agape

# BATHTUBS AND SHOWERS

© Stone Forest

## 100

Sculptured bathtubs—like these made from marble and black granite—need open spaces to let their true splendor shine through.

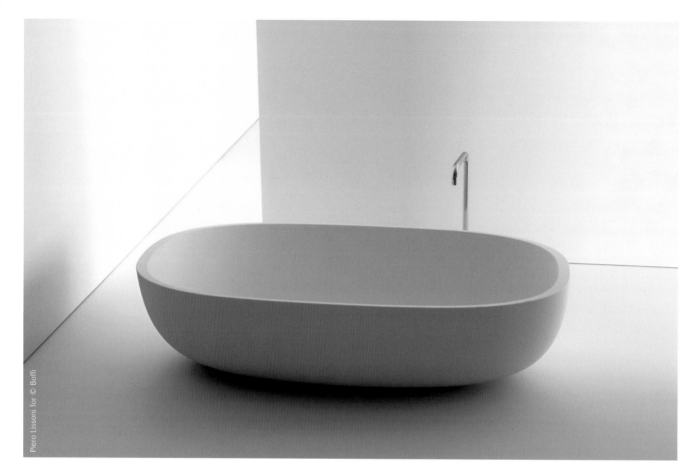

## 101

Free-standing bathtubs take
up the same space as those
built into walls, and are more
attractive.

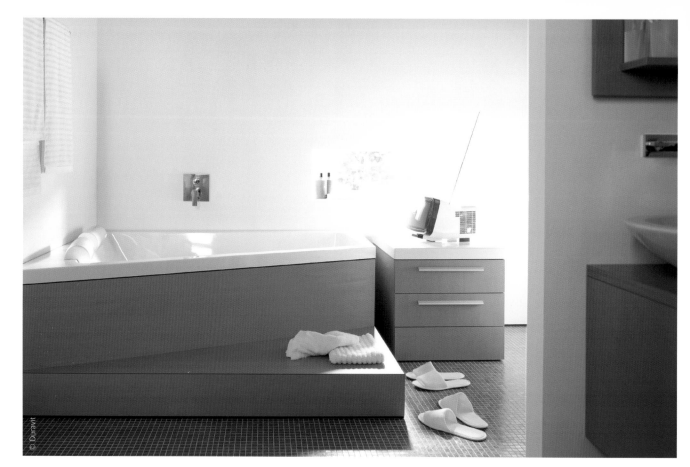

© Duravit

## 102

The wood decking marks
out the bathroom's relaxation
zone.

© Duravit

## 103

To feel just like you are in a spa, nothing beats a whirlpool bath in which you can fully submerge yourself.

© Produits Neptune

## 104

In addition to their practicality, accessories such as headrests, trims and shelving in the shower are a great way to personalize bathtubs.

© Produits Neptune

105

Wood bathtubs are aesthetically pleasing, warm to the touch and can hold a large volume of water.

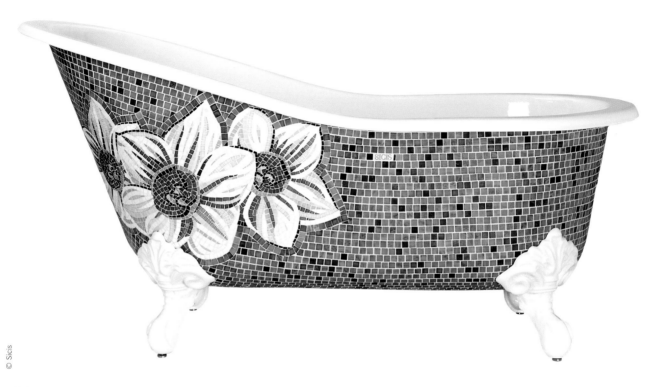

## 106

Mosaic is back in fashion. And it is moving away from its traditional uses to give new shape and color to all kinds of objects.

© Sicis

## 107

Sophisticated and extremely modern, this bathtub is ideal for giving a touch of glamour to a bathroom dominated by the color white and pure forms.

## 108

A true sculpture in opaque
stone, the Arca bathtub is
ideal for open-plan bathrooms
with a bathing zone.

## 109

This bathtub works with all bathroom styles, thanks to the pureness of its texture and its austere geometry.

## 110

The Sundeck bathtub adapts to any space with a water hook-up. When covered, the water stays hot and the tub becomes a comfortable sun lounger.

© Duravit

111

The real wood paneling in the bathroom is damp-resistant and is reminiscent of Nordic saunas.

## 112

New materials mean bathtubs are escaping from the traditional prevalence of white as more colors can now be used, along with a wider range of other décor options.

© Kaldewei

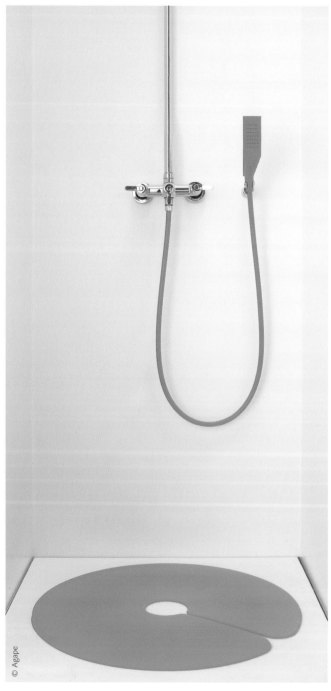

© Agape

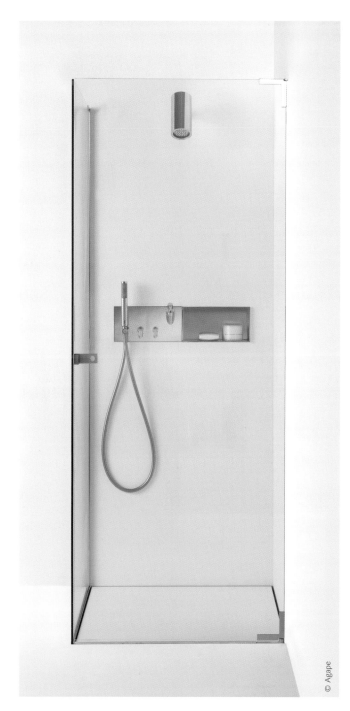

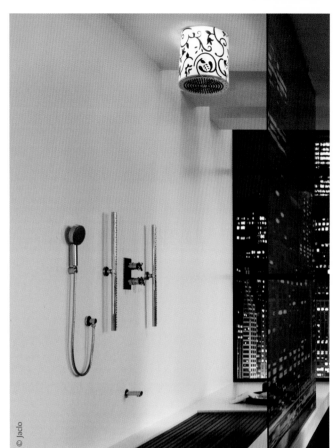

© Jaclo

© Cosentino

## 113

A lamp-and-showerhead in one, this original model gives a decorative touch to showers.

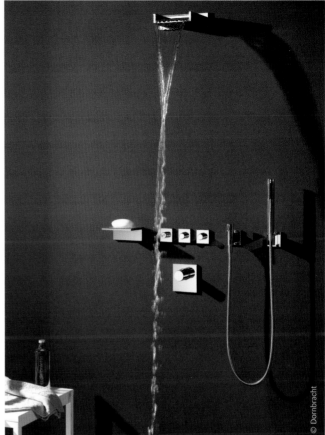

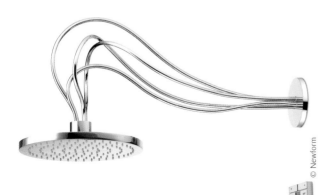

© Grup Gamma

© Dornbracht

© Newform

© Newform

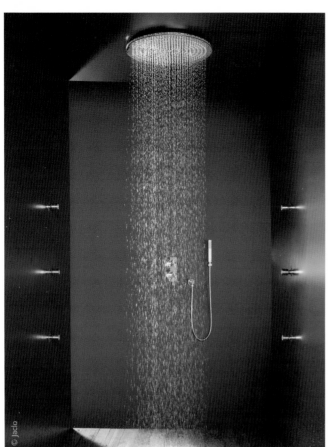

## 114

With more than 360 outlet holes, these showerheads create a relaxing rainfall effect.

## 115

Advanced showerhead technology has meant showering can now be a more relaxing experience. Not only do these showerheads eject water, but also light and aromas.

© Duravit

# FIXTURES

David Chipperfield for © Roca

116

Bathroom fixtures and fittings must be in harmony with the overall style of the space.

117

When suites are dominated by natural colors, bathroom fixtures and fittings are ideal for creating contrasts.

## 118

Bathrooms can be livened up by using accessories that break away from traditional whites.

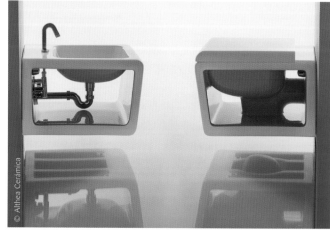

© Althea Cerámica

## 119

Basic geometry is applied to the shape of the WC. Push-button bidets use less water.

## 120

Perfect for smaller spaces,
this ceramic unit incorporates
the washbasin, shelving and
a towel rack.

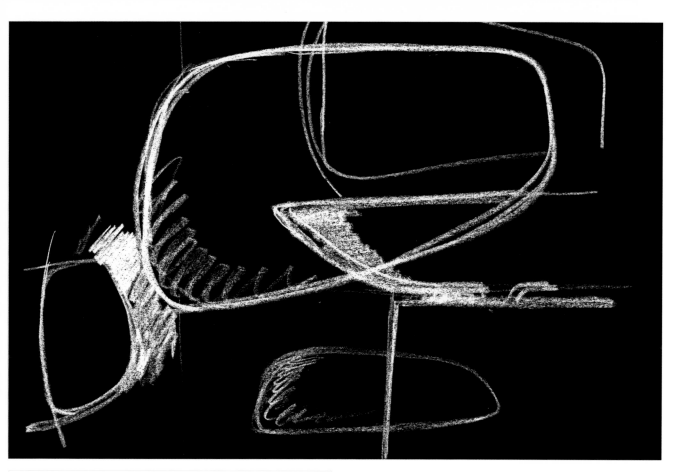

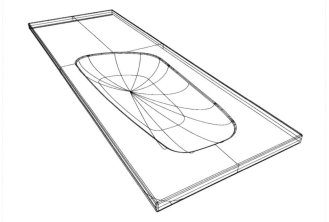

121

The stylish washbasin imitates natural forms, transforming it into a classic piece that works with all styles.

122

Wood and stone are
integrated into the washbasin,
adding a natural touch to the
bathroom.

© Pomme d'Or

© Decolav

123

An unusually shaped washbasin is all that is needed to imbue individuality into bathrooms with simpler designs.

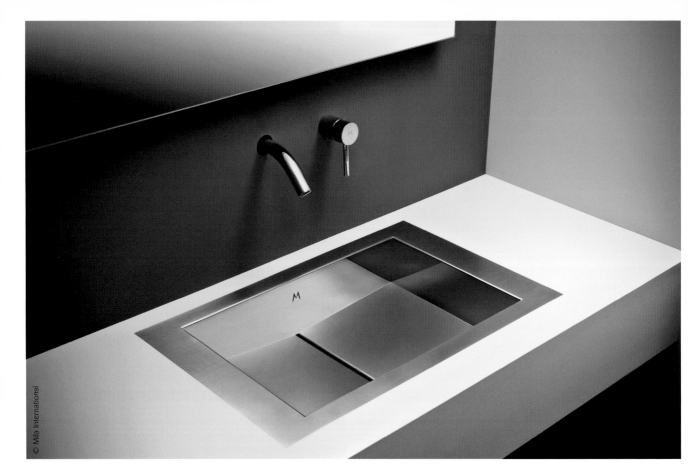

## 124

The "less is more" rule is
applied to these steel
washbasins with architectural
designs, making them perfect
for minimalist bathrooms.

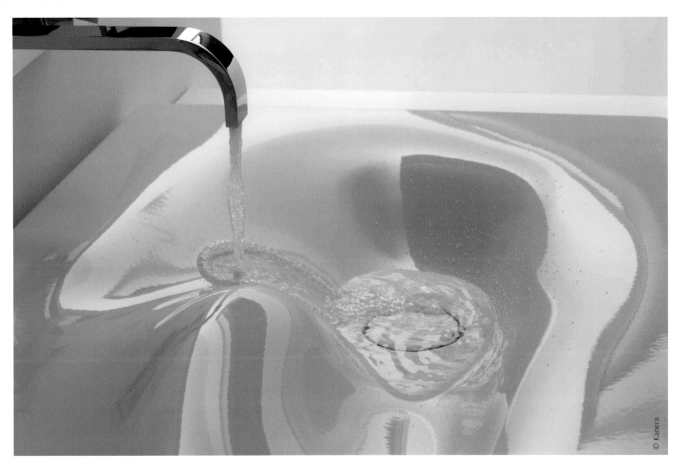

125

The washbasin easily fits into
the 6mm-wide modules with
aluminum frame. These are
from the Mondart collection,
by Gamadecor.

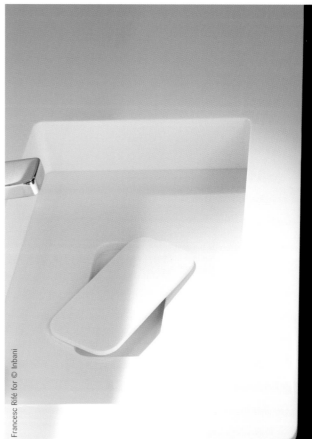

Francesc Rifé for © Inbani

© Decolav

126

Transparent glass is ideal
for bathrooms with little
natural light.

Matteo Thun for © Vitra

© Althea Ceramica

## 127

This ceramic shower base, by Matteo Thun, is a quick and easy way of changing the look of a bathroom.

## 128

Colored washbasins are a great option for bathrooms in need of a dash of originality.

© Trentino

# SURFACES

## 129

Mosaics adapt to all areas and give an appealing range of hues that enrich all surfaces.

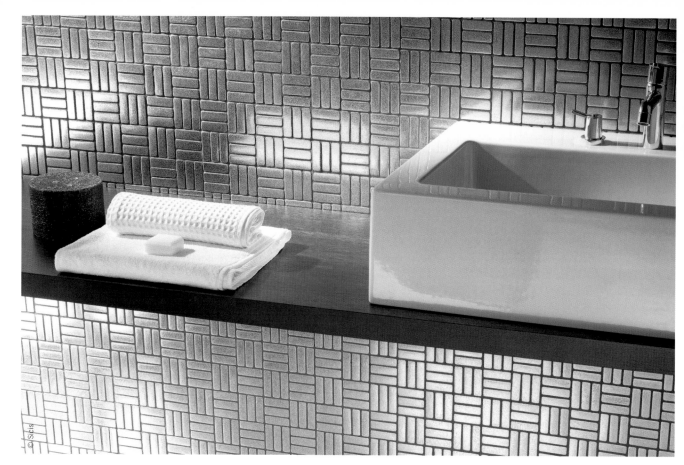

© Sicis

## 130

Metallic finishes create
modern atmospheres. They
are ideal for walls that receive
little light.

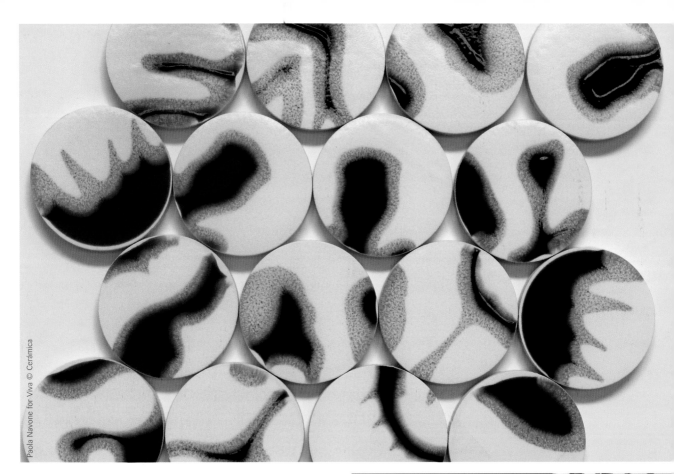

Paola Navone for Viva © Cerámica

The ceramic line Drops has
a complementary range of
bathroom fittings, fixtures and
accessories using the same
design to enable an integral
image.

Paola Navone for © Viva Cerámica

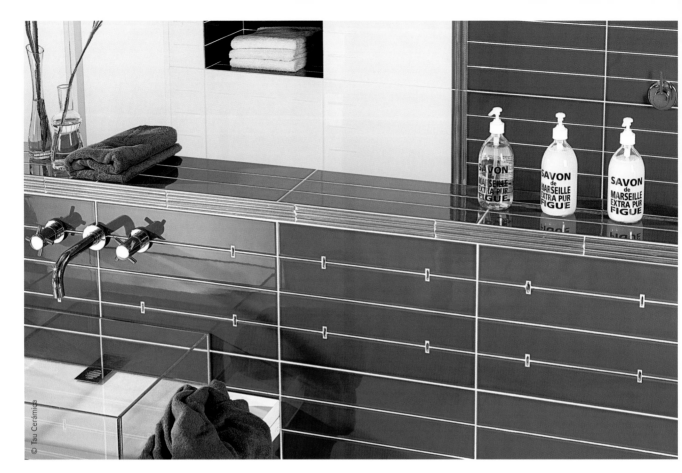

## 132

Rectangular floor tiles, such
as the Chic line, by Tau
Cerámica, visually prolong
surfaces.

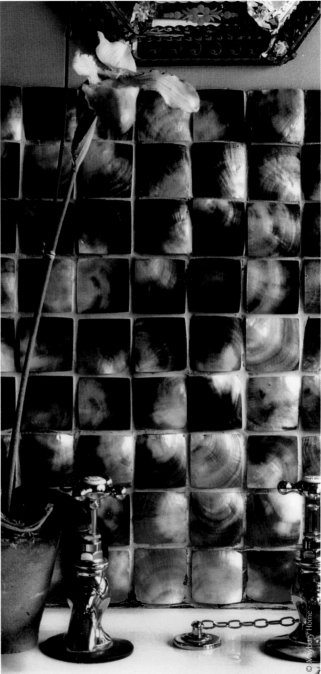

## 133

The fusion of textures and patterns generates sophisticated atmospheres. The only rule is consistency in the shades.

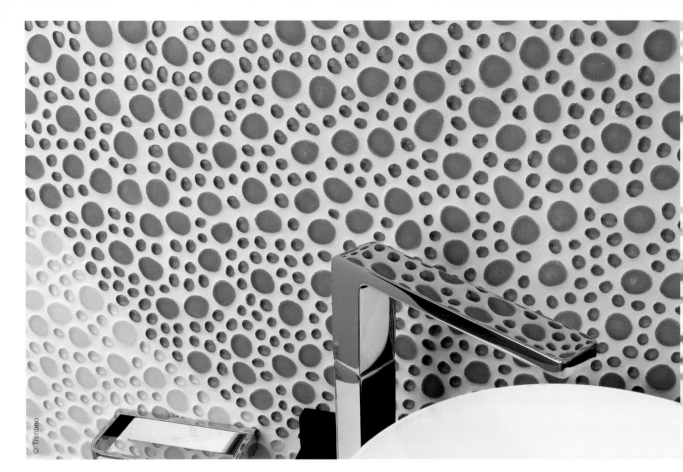

## 134

This tiling simulates the
texture of pebbles and is ideal
for water zones.

© Trentino

## 135

Ceramic surfaces that simulate skin are visually optimized when contrasted with white bathroom fixtures.

© Viva Cerámica

© Viva Cerámica

## 136

The more complex the texture of the tiling, the more simple the furnishings and the fixtures should be.

# FITTINGS
# AND ACCESSORIES

© Inda

Francesc Rifé for © Inbani

137

The hidden shelf behind the mirror helps keep walls free of clutter.

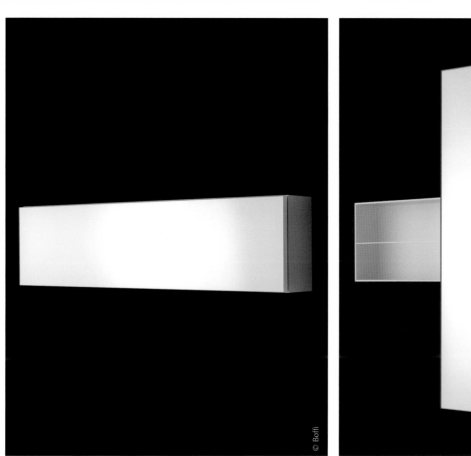

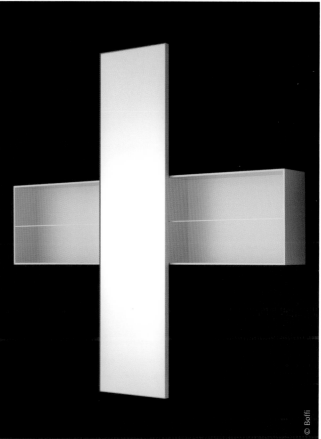

138

The functional light built into the mirror has the extra advantage of creating intimacy.

## 139

The curved-trim edging of
these mirrors contrasts
with the pure lines of the
washbasins, creating
an eye-catching quality.

© Duravit

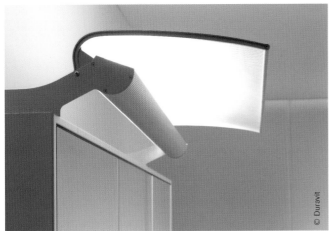

© Duravit

140

The mirror on the wall behind the washbasin creates a focal point and makes the bathroom appear larger.

## 141

The shelf above the washbasin is useful for holding the soap dish when there is a lack of space.

© Wetstyle

142

Headrests are ideal for
spending lazy hours soaking
in the tub.

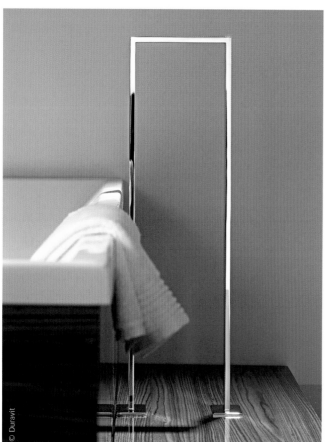

© Duravit

© Cogliati

## 143

Fitted near the bathtub or washbasin, free-standing towel holders come in a wide range of designs that form an integral part of the general aesthetics of the atmosphere.

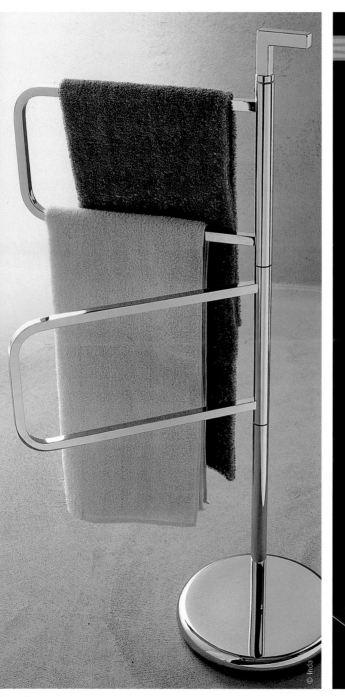

© Inda

© Inda

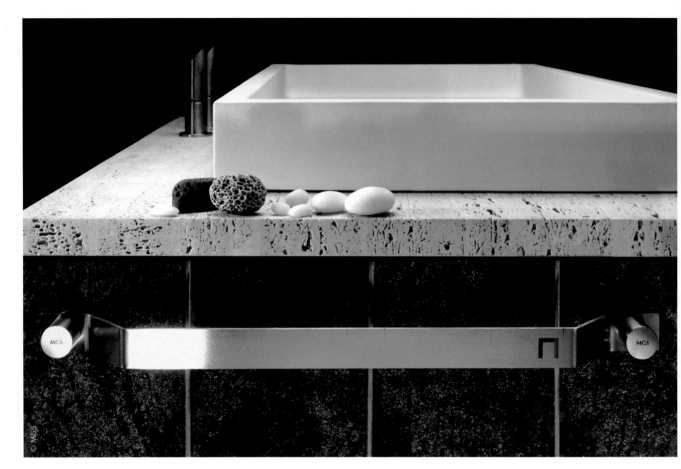

## 144

The hanging steel and leather magazine rack is an elegant solution for storing books and magazines.

## 145

Steel hangers and hooks and
polished lines can be
combined with all styles.

© Pomme d'Or

© Inda

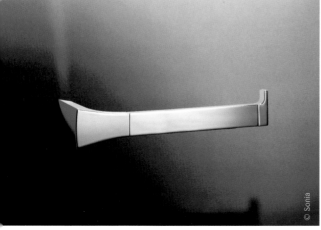

© Sonia

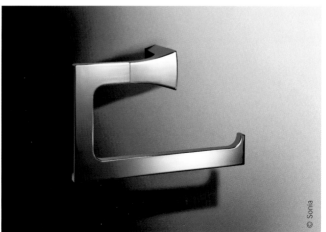

© Sonia

© Wetstyle

## 146

Using the outer part of the bathtub for shelving is a great way to gain extra storage space.

© Keuco

## 147

Industrial lines and opaque finishes are the main traits of fittings and fixtures in modern bathrooms.

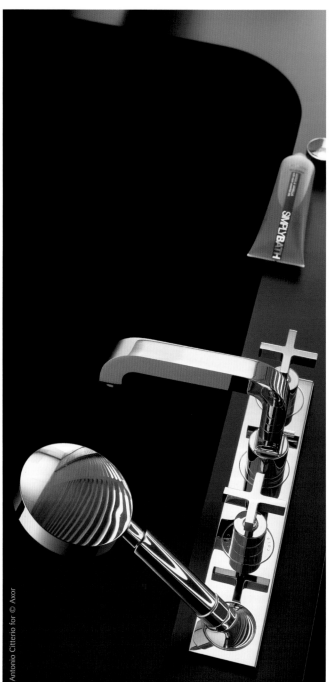

Antonio Citterio for © Axor

Antonio Citterio for © Axor

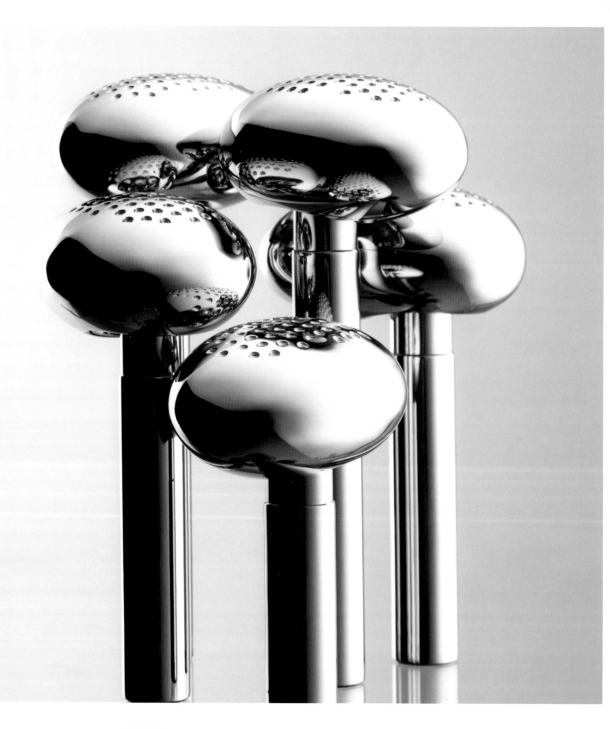

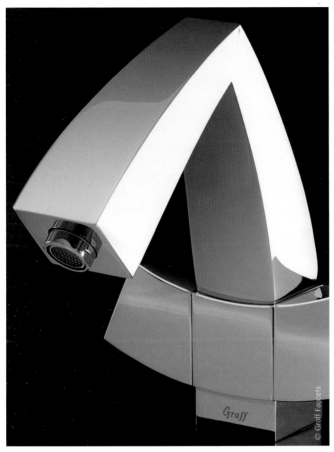

© Newform

## 148

With this faucet and control system mounted directly onto the wall, your washbasin space problems are solved.

© Graff Faucets

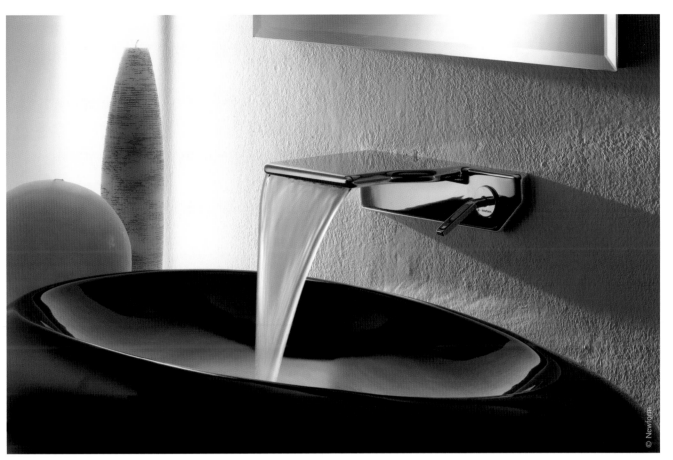

## 149

The falling water simulates a waterfall and transmits a relaxing sensation.

## 150

One-hand faucets designed
by Giulio Laccheti create
avant-garde ambience.

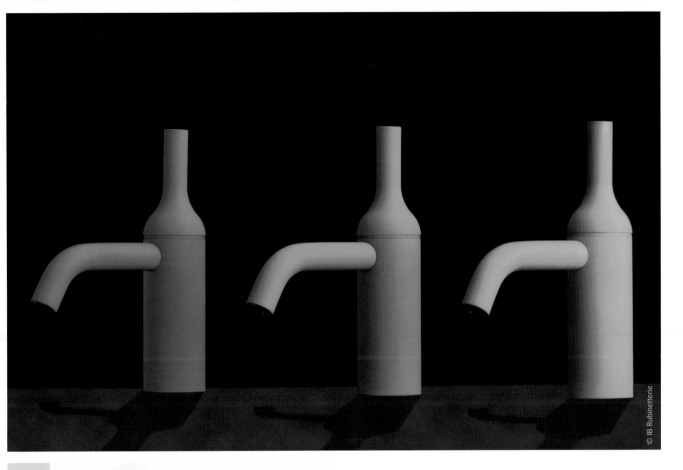

# Directory

Alonso Balaguer y Arquitectos Asociados
Roda 40
08019 Barcelona, Spain
P. +34 933 034 160
estudi@alonsobalaguer.com
www.alonsobalaguer.com

Andrée Putman
83 Avenue Denfert-Rochereau
75014 Paris, France
P. +33 155 42 88 55
contact@andreeputman.com
www.andreeputman.com

Anna Vaughan Architects
151 Bayswater Rd
Rushcutters Bay NSW 2011, Australia
P. +61 2 9361 0900
admin@annavaughanarchitects.com.au
www.annavaughanarchitects.com.au

Architectenbureau Paul de Ruiter
Leidsestraat 8-10
NL-1017 PA, Amsterdam, The Netherlands
P. +31 20 626 32 44
info@paulderuiter.nl
www.paulderuiter.nl

Architects Eat
Level 2, 227 Commercial Road
South Yarra, Victoria 3141, Australia
P. +61 3 9824 0813
www.eatas.com.au

Atelier Tekuto
301-6-15-16 Honkomagome
Bunkyo-ku, Tokyo 113-0021, Japan
P. +81 3 5940 2770
info@tekuto.com
www.tekuto.com

Carmen Barasona Comunicación e
Interiorismo
Pelfort 20, casa 3
08017 Barcelona, Spain
P. +34 607 221 321
cbarasona@telefonica.net
www.barasona.com

Cindy Rendely Architexture
44 Charles Street West, nº 2504
Toronto, Canada M4Y1R7
P. +1 416 924 9696
cindy@crarchitexture.com
www.crarchitexture.com

CJ Studio
Floor 6 No 54, Lane 260 Kwang Fu
South Road
Taipei, Taiwan
P. +886 2 2773-8366
cj@shi-chieh-lu.com
www.shi-chieh-lu.com

Coy + Yiontis Architects
Level 2, 387 Clarendon Street
South Melbourne 3205, Victoria, Australia
P. +61 3 9645 7600
cy@cyarchitects.com.au
www.cyarchitects.com.au

Cream
10/F 88 Hing Fat Street
Causeway Bay, Hong Kong
P. +852 2147 1297
info@cream.com.hk
www.cream.com.hk

David Luck Architecture
7 Hardy Street South Yarra 3141, Australia
P. +61 3 986 77509
www.users.bigpond.com/david.luck

EX-IT Architecture
Kloostestraat 33
9120 Beveren, Belgium
P. +32 3 755 36 30
mail@ex-it.be
www.ex-it.be

Filip Deslee
Kronenburgstraat 27 bus 211
2000 Antwerp, Belgium
info@ filipdeslee.com
www.filipdeslee.com

Filippo Bombace
1, Via Monte Tomatico
00141 Rome, Italy
P. +39 06 868 98266
info@filippobombace.com
www.filippobombace.com

Fougeron Architecture
431 Tehama Street, Suite 1
San Francisco, CA 94103, USA
P. +1 415 641 5744
anne@fougeron.com
www.fougeron.com

**FRAP**
Biartstraat 33
2018 Antwerp, Belgium
P. +32 3 237 16 74
architecture@frap.be
www.frap.be

**García & Ruiz**
Antonio Acuña 14, 2ºB
28009 Madrid, Spain
P. +34 915 774 518
ggrv@nauta.es
www.ggrvarquitectos.com

**Greg Natale Design**
Studio 6, level 3, 35 Buckimgham Street
Surry Hills NSW 2010, Australia
P. +61 2 8399 2103
info@gregnatale.com
www.gregnatale.com

**Griffin Enright Architects**
12468 Washington Blvd
Los Angeles, CA 90066, USA
P. +1 310 391 4484
info@griffinenrightarchitects.com
www.griffinenrightarchitects.com

**Gwenael Nicolas/Curiosity**
2-13-16 Tomigaya, Shibuya-Ku, Tokyo
151-0063, Japan
P. +81 03 5452 0095
info@curiosity.jp
www.curiosity.jp

**Ippolito Fleitz Group**
Augustenstrasse 87
70197 Stuttgart, Germany
P. +49 711 993392 330
info@ifgroup.org
www.ifgroup.org

**ITN Architects International**
54 Glasshouse Road
Collingwood Victoria 3066, Australia
P. +61 3 9416 3883
zvi@itnarchitects.com
www.itnarchitects.com

**Jean Pierre Heurteau Design**
781 High St, Armadale
Victoria 3143, Australia
P. +61 3 9576 1349

**Jaime Rouillon arquitectura**
Postal. 7-1580 San Jose
1000 Costa Rica
P. +506 2222 7045
jrouillon@rouillonarquitectura.com
www.rouillonarquitectura.com

**Joan Dot**
Carrer del Ter 50
08570 Torelló, Spain
P. +34 938 504 646
joandot@joandot.com
www.joandot.com

**Joan Pons Forment**
Lull 47, ático 4
08005 Barcelona, Spain
P. +34 670 856 261
ponsforment@coac.net

**Jordi Galí Estudi**
Passatge Forasté 4, entr D
08022 Barcelona, Spain
P. +34 932 115 442
jg@jgaliestudi.com
www.jgaliestudi.com

**Jordi Garcés**
D'en Quintana 4, 2
08002 Barcelona, Spain
P. +34 933 173 188
jordigarces@jordigarces.com
www.jordigarces.com

**Jorge Queralt Gironés**
Gran de Gràcia 103, 1º 1ª
08012 Barcelona, Spain
P. +34 666 922 525
jorgequeralt@yahoo.es

**Jorge Subietas**
Bruc 6, 08010 Barcelona, Spain
P. +34 932 680 562
interiorismo@jorgesubietas.com
www.jorgesubietas.com

**Kevin Van Volcem**
Singel 10, 8200 Brugge, Belgium
P. +32 50 688806
architect@kevinvanvolcem.be
www.kevinvanvolcem.be

**Landau + Kindelbacher**
Thierschstrasse 17
80538 Munich, Germany
P. +49 892422 890
info@landaukindelbacher.de
www.landaukindelbacher.de

Lizarriturry Tuneu Arquitectura
Castell 6
17256 Palau Sator, Girona, Spain
P. +34 972 634 119
lita@coac.net
www.lizarriturry.com/arquitectura

Marais Design
105, 1F, nº 32, Aalley 8, Lane 36, sec. 5
East Road Ming-Sheng,Taipei, Taiwan
P. +886 287874097

Marcel Wanders
Westerstraat 187
1015 MA Amsterdam, The Netherlands
P. +31 20 422 13 39
joy@marcelwanders.com
www.marcelwanders.com

MarS Architects
97 Linden Street
Oakland, CA 94607, USA
P. +1 510 663 2144
info@marsarchitects.com
www.marsarchitects.com

McIntosh Poris Associates
36801 Woodward Avenue, Suite 200
Birmingham, MI 48009, USA
P. +1 248 258 9346
mp@mcintoshporis.com
www.mcintoshporis.com

McLauchlan and Associates
430 Huntingdale Rd
Mt. Waverley, Victoria 3149, Australia
P. +61 3 9888 3444
robmac@mclauchlan.com.au
www.mclauchlan.com.au

Meritxell Cuartero Cavallé / Dt6 Arquitectes
Torres 2, bxos. 2a
08012 Barcelona, Spain
P. +34 934 766 575
mcuartero@dt6arq.cat
www.dt6arq.cat

Michael P. Johnson Design Studios
PO Box 4058 Cave Creek
AZ 85327, USA
P. +1 480 488 2692
michael@mpjstudio.com
www.mpjstudio.com

MoHen Design International
No. 18, Alley 396, Wulumuqi S. Rd. 200031
Shanghai, China
P. +86 21 64370910/64374175/64374462
mohen@mohen-design.com
www.mohen-design.com

NAP Architects
2-15-7-1F Sakura-Shinmachi Setagaya-ku
154-0015 Tokyo, Japan
P. +81 3 5426 0105
nakamura@nakam.info
www.nakam.info

Nicholas Murray Architects
7 Hotham Street
South Melbourne, VIC 3205, Australia
P. +61 3 9686 0718
nicholas@nma.net.au
www.nma.net.au

Nico Heysse
Deneckstraat 22
1081 Brussels, Belgium
P. +32 476 31 09 68
nicoheysse@skynet.be

Nixon Tulloch Fortey Architecture
98 Balmain Street, Cremorne
Victoria 3121, Australia
P. +61 3 9429 3200
melb@ntfarchitecture.com.au
www.ntfarchitecture.com.au

Octavio Mestre
Ps. Sant Joan 84, ppal. 1
08009 Barcelona, Spain
P. +34 934 577 338
octaviomestre@coac.net
www.octaviomestre.com

ONA Arquitectes
www.onaarquitectes.com

One Plus Partnership Limited
9/F, New Wing, Sing Pao Building
101 King's Road
North Point, Hong Kong
P. +852 25919308
admin@onepluspartnership.com
www.onepluspartnership.com

Project Orange
2nd Floor, Block E, Morelands
5-23 Old Street, London EC1V 9HL, UK
P. +44 20 7566 0410
mail@projectorange.com
www.projectorange.com

Rahel Belatchew Arkitektur
Regeringsgatan 88
111 39 Stockholm, Sweden
P. +46 8 55 80 14 14
www.rbarkitektur.se

Sally Draper Architects
Suite 1 45 Watkins St
Fitzroy North, Victoria 3068, Australia
P. +61 3 9486 6606

Sixx design
www.sixxdesign.com

Slade Arquitecture
150 Broadway 807
New York, NY 10038, USA
P. +1 212 677 6380
info@sladearch.com
www.sladearch.com

SR Constructors
Paris, 188 bis
08036 Barcelona, Spain
P. +34 932 922 262
info@srpromotors.com
www.srpromotors.com

Stanic Harding
123 Commonwealth Street, Surry Hills
NSW, 2010, Australia
P. +61 2 9211 6710
architects@stanicharding.com.au
www.stanicharding.com

Stephen Jolson
58 Greville St
Prahran 3181 Victoria, Australia
P. +61 3 8656 7100
mail@jolson.com.au
www.sjarchitect.com

The Apartment
213 West 23rd, 7th, 8th floor
New York, NY 10012, USA
P. +1 212 219 3661
www.theapt.com

Verdickt & Verdickt Architects
Oranjestraat 44
B-2060 Antwerp, Belgium
P. +32 3 233 83 51
info@verdicktenverdickt.be
www.www.verdicktenverdickt.be

Victor Cañas/Cañas Arquitectos
PO Box 340 2050
San Pedro Montes de Oca, Costa Rica
P. +506 2253 2112
victor@canas.co.cr
victor.canas.co.cr

BRANDS

Agape
Moss. 150 Greene St.
New York, NY 10012, USA
P. +1 212 204 7100
www.mossonline.com
www.agapedesign.it

Alessi
30 E. 60th St.
New York, NY 10022, USA
P. +1 212 317 9880
www.alessi.com

Antonio Lupi Design
www.antoniolupi.it

Aquatic Industries
P. +1 800 555 5324
www.aquaticwhirlpools.com

Artquitect
www.artquitect.net

Axor
Hansgrohe USA
1490 Bluegrass Lakes Parkway
Alpharetta, GA 30004, USA
P. +1 800 488 8119
www.axor-design.com

Bisazza
43 Green Street
New York, NY 10013, USA
P. +1 212 334 7130
bisazza.newyork@bisazzausa.com
www.bisazza.com

Brasstech
2001 East Carnegie Ave
Santa Ana, CA 92705-5531, USA
P. +1 949 417 5207
info@brasstech.com
www.brasstech.com

Boffi
www.boffi.com

Boxart
www.boxart.org

Ceramica Althea
www.altheaceramica.it

Ceramica Flaminia
www.ceramicaflaminia.it

Cogliati
www.cogliati-cogliati.it

Cosentino
13124 Trinity Drive
Stafford, TX 77477, USA
P. +1 281 4947277
silestone@cosentinousa.com
www.cosentinogroup.net

Decolav
424 SW, 12th Ave
Deerfied Beach, FL 33442, USA
P. +1 561 274 2110
www.decolav.com

Dornbracht
1700 Executive Drive South
Suite 600, Duluth, GA 30096, USA
P. +1 800 774 1181
mail@dornbracht.com
www.dornbracht.com

Duravit
2205 Northmont Parkway, Suite 200
Duluth, GA 30096, USA
P. +1 770 9313575
info@usa.duravit.com
www.duravit.us

Gamadecor
www.gama-decor.com

Gessi
13037 Serravalle
Sesia, Vercelli, Italia
P. +39 0163 544111
www.gessi.it

Graff Faucets
3701 W. Burnham Street
Milwaukee, WI 53215, USA
P. +1 800 954 4723
customerservice@graff-faucets.com
www.graff-faucets.com

Grup Gamma
www.gamma.es

IB Rubinetterie
www.ibrubinetterie.it

Inbani
www.inbani.com

Inda
ww.inda.net

Jaclo
129 Dermody Street
Cranford, NJ 07016, USA
P. +1 800 852 3906
www.jaclo.com

Kanera
www.kanera.de

Keuco
935 A Cedar Drive
Newton, NJ 07860, USA
P. +1 973 383 7500
www.keuco.de

Kohler
P. +1 800 456 4537
www.us.kohler.com

Laufen
11190 NW 25th Street, Suite 100
Miami, FL 33172, USA
P. +800 321 0684
info.tilegroup@rocatilegroup.com
www.laufen.com

Maybury
www.mayburyhome.com

MGS Designs
20423 State Rd. 7, #F6-291
Boca Raton, FL 33498, USA
P. +1 561 218 8798
info@mgsdesigns.com
www.mgsdesigns.com

Mila-International
20 W 21st, Suite 804
New York, NY 10010, USA
P. +1 646 415 8666
www.Mila-International.com

Moen
P. +1 800 289 6636
www.moen.com

Neo-Metro
15125 Proctor Ave
City of Industry, CA 91746, USA
P. +1 800 591 9050
www.neo-metro.com

Newform
www.newform.it

Oceanside
info@glasstile.com
www.glasstile.com

Pomme D'Or
www.blanchcristal.com

Porcelanosa Grupo
1970 New Highway
Farmingdale, NY 11735, USA
P. +1 631 845 7070
www.porcelanosa.com

Produits Neptune
6835, Rue Plcard, Saint-Hyacinthe
Québec, Canada J2S 1H3
P. +1 450 773 7058
info@neptuneweb.com
www.bainsneptune.com

Ramón Soler
www.ramonsoler.net

Regia
www.regiasrl.it

Roca
11190 NW 25th Street, Suite 100
Miami, FL 33172, USA
P. +1 800 321 0684
info.tilegroup@rocatilegroup.com

Sicis
470 Broome Street
New York, NY 10013, USA
P. +1 212 965 4100
www.sicis.com

Smallbone of Devizes
135 East 65th Street
New York, NY 10021, USA
P. +1 212 288 3454
www.smallbone.co.uk

Sonia
Blackman Manhattan Showroom
85 Fifth Ave., Second Floor
New York, NY, USA
P. +1 212 337 1000
www.sonia-sa.com

Stone Forest
213, S. St. Francis Drive
Santa Fe, NM 87501, USA
P. +1 888 682 2987
stoneforest@drs-associates.com
www.stoneforest.com

Surface Tiles
www.surfacetiles.com

Tau Cerámica
www.tauceramic.net

Trentino
www.trentino.es

Villeroy & Boch
www.villeroy-boch.com

Vitra USA
305 Shawnee N. Drive, Suite 600
Suwanee, GA 30024, USA
P. +1 770 904 6830
www.vitra-usa.com

Viva Cerámica
www.cerviva.it

Wetstyle
276 Saint-Jacques
Montreal, QC, Canada H2Y 1N3
info@wetstyle.ca
P. +1 866 842 1367
www.wetstyle.ca

Zazzeri
www.zazzeri.it